COLLECT RENT, DON'T PAY IT!

A BEGINNER'S GUIDE TO RENTAL PROPERTY INVESTING

Norm Spivey
National Certified Counselor (NCC)
Colonel, US Army (Retired)

© Norman D. Spivey, 2022

No reproduction of any part may take place without written permission.

First Published 2022

ISBN 978-1-7352159-4-5 (Paperback)
ISBN 978-1-7352159-5-2 (eBook)

I dedicate this book to my family.
We could not have come as far as we have without the love
and dedication of family.

Contents

Why Rental Properties? 1
Setting the Conditions 17
    Establish Goals for the Investment
    Complete Initial Market Analysis
    Get Financing Set and Ready
    Find the Yes
    Determine Acceptable Risk and Make a Commitment
    Establish Core Values and Business Practices
Selecting the Best Property 35
    To Use a Buyer's Agent or Not
    Location, Location, Location
    Determine Capitalization Rate for a Potential Property
    Have the Property Professionally Inspected
    To Build or Buy
    Setting Rent and Security Deposits
Establishing a Relationship With Tenants 58
    Advertising and Showing
    Screening
    Signing the Lease
    Keeping Tenants Content
    Collecting Rent
    Managing Bad Tenants
Maintain the Investment 84
    Repairs, Maintenance and Improvements
    When to Repair and Maintain
    Learn how to do it yourself
Bookkeeping and Taxes 98
    Financials
    Maintain Receipts and a Ledger

      Leveraging the Tax Benefits of Real Estate
      Capital Gains Tax and Depreciation Recapture
Grow and Secure your Business 119
      To Form a LLC or Not
      Insuring the Investment
      Refinancing
      Hiring a Property Manager
Final Thoughts 136

Disclaimers

The information provided in this book is for informational purposes only and is not intended to be a source of advice. The information contained in this book does not constitute financial advice and should never be used without first consulting with a financial professional to determine what may be best for your individual needs.

The views, opinions and biases expressed are the authors and do not reflect those of the U.S. Army or the Department of Defense.

Chapter 1: Why Rental Properties?

There is no better way for the average person to grow net worth than owning real estate. I'd even go so far as calling it a financial truth required to build wealth. There are some who would argue this point and I'll gladly take on the debate. One thing is for sure, paying rent an entire adult life will make it more difficult to get ahead and increase net worth. Why not get a return on that rent money instead of improving a landlord's net worth? Be the landlord, not the tenant!

So what makes real estate, specifically rental properties, such a great investment? While the red hot rental market we have today and uncertain stock market should be all the rationale one needs to make the plunge into rental property investing, I'll offer three additional reasons rental property is a smart move for any investor.

Real Estate Increasing in Value is Simply a Matter of "Physics"

The stock of tech companies, service providers, even commodities may ebb or flow in value, but land and real estate almost always increases. There is no more land being produced and as long as birth rates generally outpace death rates, inhabitants of our planet will always need a place to stay. Of course, there are exceptions to the rule, if the county decides to put in a landfill right next to a property, then all bets are off! But negative factors impacting the value of real estate are the exception rather than the rule. Real estate increasing in value is a safe bet.

Rental Properties Offer a Better Return on Investment in the Long Run

I'll offer some math to back up my assertion. First, let's look at $50,000 invested in a taxable investment account. We'll assume a very generous 5% annual return after advisor fees and taxes compounded over 20 years. In 20 years that $50,000 will have grown to almost $132,000! Not too shabby, right?

Now let's look at $50,000 used as a down payment on a $200,000 duplex held for 20 years. We will assume a 4% interest rate on the $150,000 loan principle amortized over 30 years. We'll also assume that rents for the two units will increase at the same rate as expenses (specifically taxes, insurance and maintenance costs) so we will keep the net income constant over 20 years. Bear with me, the math is a little more complicated.

Monthly Income	
Gross Rent	$1,800
Mortgage (P&I)	($716)
Insurance	($100)
Property Taxes	($333)
Operating Costs	($200)
Net Income	$451

$451 per month in net income times 240 months is $108,240 pretax. That's over $20,000 less than our investment account! But wait, let suppose we fight the urge to spend that hard earned extra $451 per month and throw it in that same taxable investment account with the 5% annual return. Suddenly, that rental income over 20 years jumps from $108,240 to over $183,000!

And there is still more to be made on this initial $50,000 investment. We can't forget about appreciation in value of the property! We'll assume a modest 2% annual appreciation which is lower than average. In 20 years the duplex has appreciated in value to a little over $297,000. Assuming we still owe the bank about $65,000 in principle on the loan, that means we've made an additional $182,000 in equity above our down payment of $50,000! Important to point out here, it was our tenants who paid down our principle and built that equity for us!

All told, the return on an initial $50,000 investment in a duplex is $365,000 pre-tax! That is a 700% growth on our initial investment in 20 years compared to 260% if the $50,000 was placed in a taxable investment account making 5%!

"I notice you said, pre-tax". Glad you noticed! The tax advantages of rental income are many and we'll cover in detail during an upcoming chapter. Regardless, any tax implications over the years for the $365,000 would not come close to equaling the $233,000 difference between the two options. Which leads me to the third reason why real estate is a smart move.

When Actively Managed, Rental Properties are a Less Risky Investment than Mutual Funds or Equities

The IRS definition of rental income as "passive" is completely misleading. I will say it several times throughout this book, investing in and managing rental properties is a business. Key words here are "actively managed". If actively managed, much of the risk associated with rental property investing is mitigated and overall less than the risk we encounter when entrusting a financial advisor or fund manager to grow our hard earned money for us. We'll cover growing and securing our real estate investment as well as tax implications in later chapters.

At this point it is probably worthy to look at exactly how one profits from rental property investing. This is the essence of the material we'll cover for the next 100 pages!

Rental Income. How much income a property will produce depends on numerous variables. Regardless, a good investment property should produce some level of income, meaning that the monthly rents collected should equal more than the outgo for mortgages, insurance, taxes, maintenance and any other expenses. The IRS will refer to real estate income as passive. I assure you, nothing is "passive" about real estate investing! From the moment of first viewing a listing when shopping for properties to picking up the monthly rent check, every aspect of real estate investing involves a decision or action. This will become crystal clear as we cover the ins and outs of rental property investing. Think of it as a part time job and it won't sting as bad when receiving that call from an angry tenant about a broken HVAC. Ideally, any net rental income is rolled back into a taxable investment account or tax deferred retirement account which makes the profits compound even more as explained in the earlier example.

Building Equity. This is my personal favorite and can be maximized in several ways. Simply put, equity is the difference between what the property is worth and how much is owed to the bank. Essentially, a portion of monthly collected rent checks pass through the investor to the bank paying down principal and thusly building equity. Additionally, property values will almost always increase. Multi-family property value won't increase as quickly as single family homes but will increase nonetheless. There are also "sweat equity" improvements a property owner can complete to improve the condition of a property making it more valuable. Obviously, the more sweat equity an owner can do on their own, the more return on the improvement.

Tax Benefits. There are tax advantages to owning real estate which we will cover in detail later. In a way, the tax benefits of rental income make it similar to the tax benefits offered by investing in a 401k, sort of a "pre-tax" benefit. Although a landlord may collect $10,000 in gross rental income for example, after deducting expenses and depreciation the actual taxable income is MUCH lower. These tax savings add up over time and increase the "earning" power of a rental property investment portfolio.

So why do so many people continue to pay rent and avoid taking the plunge into real estate? There are times in our lives when we have to pay rent due to work or other circumstances. I've paid tens of thousands in rent money over the years and who knows, in my senior years I may find myself paying rent again. Others may choose to live in a high cost area of the nation where it is near impossible to buy real estate except for the most wealthy of earners. Personally, I would consider moving!

Also, there are two major hurdles that have to be overcome before one can dive into real estate. First, with only a few exceptions I'll review in a later chapter, investing in real estate requires capital for a down payment. Usually this is equal to 20-25% of the purchase price.

Similarly, to borrow money at competitive rates for a real estate purchase, one usually needs a credit score of around 700 or better. If poor decisions or other circumstances earlier in life have wrecked a credit score, it will take some time and discipline to repair. Unfortunately, this may require paying rent a little longer until credit gets back up into the good range, but home ownership is still within grasp.

All that being said, my assumption is most people don't invest in real estate simply out of fear for the personal and financial commitment real estate investing requires.

Coupled with this is a natural fear of the unknown and inherent risks. Most people assume investing in real estate is a risky endeavor and it certainly can be, but as stated, with active management, the risk in real estate is mitigated. My hope is through this book, I can put some of those fears to rest and make owning real estate an important part of your investment portfolio!

The dynamic of real estate ownership has changed quite a bit in just the last 20 years. From the mid-1960s, to the 1990s, owning real estate required substantial cash on hand. This was due to mortgage rates often topping 10%! To buy a home, one had to have a sizeable down payment or the monthly mortgage payments would be out of reach for many workers. This century has seen bank loan interest rates remain at or below the 5% mark. This opened the door (pun intended) for workers to buy their own homes and more importantly invest in real estate.

Home ownership and real estate investing is a long term position. To purchase a property, most of us will have to get a mortgage for 15 to 30 years. To illustrate how lower bank loan rates have fundamentally changed real estate investing and put home ownership within many peoples reach, let's look at the principle and interest for a $200,000 mortgage (in today's dollars) at 10% and 5% interest rates over 30 years.

| $200,000 amortized over 30 years ||
Loan Interest Rate	Monthly Payment (principle and interest)
10%	$1755
5%	$1074

The payment, at a 10% interest rate, is nearly $700 more per month! Add to the monthly principle and interest payment, the property taxes, (typically around 2% of the home's value per year), maintenance and upkeep costs as well as homeowner's insurance and it is easy to see why real estate ownership was out of reach for most workers just a few years ago.

Thankfully, interest rates in the 5% or lower range have been here for a while and hopefully we will never go back to 10% or greater mortgage rates. Many people have been able to take advantage of this opportunity over the past 20 years. With the exception of a few recession periods, home ownership is steadily increasing thus far in the 21st century. This has fundamentally changed our society for the better.

Which brings me to an important point of clarification. The focus of this book, the real estate investing we'll examine, is rental properties both single and multifamily. I don't have any experience in developing raw land, flipping homes and commercial properties. I would venture a guess that many of the principles I'll cover in this book apply equally to those types of real estate investing.

And on that note, what qualifies me to offer an opinion on rental property investing? I am certainly not a multi-billion dollar investor. What I am is an average American with a successful rental property business side hustle. My wife and I went from zero rental units to 17 in 14 years. We took about $300,000 in initial investment over a span of years and turned it into a business currently worth over $2M and producing $60,000 a year net income. Small potatoes by some standards and I will be the first to admit I still have a lot to learn, but overall I'd say we've been pretty successful.

To reiterate, investing in real estate and managing properties is a part time job. It takes a lot of sacrifice which we will talk about at length in this book. That being said, my goal is to share what we've learned through our experiences, the good and the bad, to hopefully help another average American reach their financial goals. Before I do, let me introduce a little more about our own personal journey to provide some background on how and why we embarked on this real estate adventure.

Our Real Estate Journey

Many of us Generation X folk were brought up as children in the 70s and 80s experiencing residual impact from the economic hardships of the Great Depression. Our grandparents, especially those of us raised in rural areas of the South, were forever shaped (some may say scarred) by the abstract poverty they experienced during the Depression. They truly knew what it meant to go without, not just the pleasant things in life, but basics to include good nutrition and public services. If there was anything positive to come of this experience, our grandparents could literally stretch a penny into a nickel and they mastered the art of living frugally.

For their children (Generation X's parents), the Baby Boomer generation experienced new found economic security as the middle class grew during the boom times of the 50s and early 60s. Yet many of our parents who grew up witnessing their own parent's frugalness, were excellent savers themselves. This enabled many of these boomers to send my generation to college, provide basic needs reasonably well and build retirement accounts on a never before seen scale.

My family and upbringing was definitely molded in this context. I distinctly remember my grandparents living frugally to the point of depravation. My grandmother never ran the air conditioner even on the hottest summer days in the South. My grandparents kept a garden and cooked at home, reserving dinners out for very limited special occasions. I had one grandparent that sewed her own clothes. I recall my grandparent who dressed like it was the 1960s in the 1980s, not to make a statement, but because her clothes literally were from the 1960s. Despite enduring periods of extreme poverty during the Depression when they were young, my hardworking and frugal grandparents passed from this world not owing any debt, generally financially secure and possessing a small estate to pass to their heirs.

My parents certainly did not go to the same extremes as my grandparents, but I did see some similar themes. We didn't eat out often and what we ate at home was mostly nutritious but certainly not top shelf gourmet. I watched my parents over the years save for special occasions such as an annual vacation or a new car. Major expenses were always a deliberate financial plan, never a sudden impulse. I wore my fair share of hand me downs and helped my parents do-it-yourself on the weekends around the house.

Growing up, I witnessed first-hand the value of an education, or more accurately, the struggle required to be successful without an education. My immediate family, mother, father, stepfather and grandparents were working class folk. None of them had a college degree or any specialized certifications. They all worked very hard at hourly wage jobs and eventually, earned respectable livings. My mother worked all the way until she was 67 and in her later years, when she wasn't at work, took care of my ill stepfather before he passed. She really didn't have a choice.

I hold the deepest respect for my hard working family. Their example taught me about working hard and saving money as well as set the foundation for the success my own family is enjoying today. My parents continually stressed the importance of an education. They didn't specify what that meant, most likely they didn't really know. They didn't have the same opportunities I had to seek formal education beyond high school. Unfortunately, since I grew up in the pre-529 era, they weren't able to save much for my post high school education either.

But they continually emphasized the importance. They knew if I didn't get an education, I'd have to scratch out a living the best I could like they did. I understood clearly their point, there has got to be a better way!

I share all of this because the values and views on finances I witnessed first-hand growing up certainly made a big impact on my life and why I eventually invested in real estate. Making every dollar work as hard as it can is in my DNA. I learned early on how to determine between needs and wants. Moreover, I learned that real estate ownership is a hallmark of financial success for the working person.

Sans college fund, it was up to me to figure out how to pay for college. I turned to the military. It was my great privilege and honor to serve 24 years in the United States Army. I wouldn't change a thing about my time in service, but bouncing around from post to post every two to three years, sometimes overseas, makes it a challenge to invest in real estate! During my 24 years of service I spent eight years overseas! Some service members are able to purchase homes and invest in real estate but most are not.

I was blessed to meet a partner who grew up with a similar upbringing, views on finances and a desire to invest in real estate. Similar, but she grew up over 8000 miles away in the Republic of Korea! My wife and I were able to start our real estate investing journey while I served on active duty, but it certainly wasn't easy. Both of our families had dabbled in real estate when we were growing up. Neither of us came from wealthy circumstances and what little net worth our families had amassed, came almost entirely from home ownership. We set the goal early on in our marriage to own our home and decided rental property investing would become an important part of our financial plan.

However, the Army had other plans! We married in 2001 while I was stationed in Germany, so not many opportunities to invest. When we came back to the states in 2003, my next four year assignment required that we live in on-post housing. After departing that station, my next assignment (albeit only a year) also required living on post!

In 2008 we had been married seven years, had two small children and had paid rent our whole adult lives up to that point. I was 35 years old and my wife was 38. We were ready to own a home! But again, the Army gets a vote. Our next assignment was to Ft. Hood, TX. Central Texas real estate was extremely affordable at the time due to an abundance of land and low construction cost. Unfortunately, we also learned that I would be deploying within two months after arriving to Ft. Hood!

It was at this time we made the conscious decision to make our first real estate purchase a duplex. I would be gone for the first year of our assignment to Ft. Hood so the wife and toddlers didn't need much space. The kids weren't even in school yet! City zoning in Killeen, TX resulted in an abundance of nice multi-family properties mixed in with single family neighborhoods rather than massive apartment complexes.

Additionally, our seven years of frugal living and investing in mutual funds had racked up a good bit of capital in our taxable investment account. For our first purchase, we elected not to tap my VA home loan benefit and instead put 25% down payment for the investment property. We would live in one side of the duplex and rent the other. The rental income would cover our mortgage, insurance and taxes while the portion of our pay the Army designated for housing allowance would go into our pockets, or more accurately, back into our taxable investment account!

Sounds like a no brainer right? This is where the human factor and the sacrifice of rental property ownership comes in. We were nearly 40 years old and had never owned a home. We were blessed to have risen in rank to Major which certainly didn't make us wealthy but we were comfortable. Most people in our circumstance bought lovely, new construction, single family brick homes in the area.

We instead chose to live in one side of our duplex, a 1200 square foot apartment, and put our families' long term financial well-being as the priority. My wife couldn't invite people over and when she did some of the more catty spouses would remark, "how can you live like this"? The house was tiny and we barely fit. There were a lot of tears, but we made it!

One of the upsides to deployments is it offers an opportunity to save a ton of money. This coupled with the income we were making in our first duplex enabled us to save enough to buy another duplex shortly after I returned from a yearlong deployment. We were very fortunate to find a distressed property (more on this topic later) at a great price. Even though I had to spend a week fixing it up before we could offer it for rent, this duplex has since become one of our best performers.

I got to stay home about seven months before I had to deploy again. While me being out of the picture gave the wife and kids more room in our 1200 square foot duplex home, raising two small children alone and managing two rental properties was taking its toll on her. This is when we established a great relationship with a local property management company that we still maintain today (more on property management companies later!)

With the additional income from our two duplexes and the money we were saving by me being deployed, the wife went out, on her own I might add, and found yet another duplex to purchase in the area. I arrived back from the deployment just in time to make it to closing!

We had acquired three duplexes in central Texas over a four year period in good locations and at good purchase prices. Perhaps it was beginners luck, but we were certainly hooked on rental property investing! The rental market was red hot at the time (as it remains today) and the properties were turning a profit. Perhaps it was finally time to move out of the duplex and find a nice single family home for our growing family.

But again, the Army gets a vote. We received orders for another overseas assignment. Back to renting! While we were overseas for two years, our properties in Texas continued to flourish and we re-invested the rental income into our taxable investment accounts which compounded the profits nicely. Important to point out, the aforementioned investments occurred during the recession period in the 2008-2012 timeframe. Our family finances weathered the recession with no significant issues thanks in large part to real estate. Towards the end of our overseas assignment, we received our next orders, Washington, D.C.

While we loved living in the D.C. area, we also experienced some sticker shock at the price of homes. Not knowing what the military had in store for us, we decided not to buy and paid rent yet again. This proved to be a very fortuitous decision as the Army decided to move us yet again after only one year in D.C. In a very fortunate turn, we received orders for Redstone Arsenal, in Huntsville, AL.

Huntsville's claim to fame is the Marshall Space Flight Center where much of the development on the Saturn V rockets that took Americans to the moon was completed. Huntsville truly is an oasis within the Tennessee River Valley. There are numerous large and small defense industry businesses located here which draws engineers, scientists and professionals from all over the country. Some people say there is a higher density of PhD's in Huntsville, AL than anywhere else in the nation!

On top of all that, cost of living was great and there were new home developments seemingly on every corner. In 2015 at the age of 42 we bought our first single family home! Looking around the Huntsville area, we noticed that investment properties to include small condos and multifamily duplexes were very reasonably priced. Through some good timing and creative financing we'll cover in upcoming chapters, we were able to purchase three small single family condo units, three duplexes and build a fourth in just over five years.

Unlike our investment properties in central Texas, we actively managed our north Alabama properties which ended up providing my wife with a part time job, a nice change of pace for her. She previously worked as a homemaker for most of our time in the military.

When it came time to pack up and leave again on the next military adventure, our family had reached a critical cross roads. We landed, quite by accident, in a portion of the country that had a lot to offer. Our kids were at the age where friends are everything and they liked the schools. We had already invested heavily in local area real estate. Post military jobs were plentiful. Although it was a tough decision, it just made sense for our family to get off the military train after 24 years of service.

When we retired in 2019 our real estate portfolio included our personal residence, three duplexes in Texas, three duplexes and three condos in North Alabama. In 2021 we completed construction on our fourth duplex in the North Alabama area. 17 rental units in total across 10 properties in two states!

In just under 15 years we amassed are enjoying over a 600% growth on our initial investment. Important to note, "initial investment" is a bit misleading. Really only maybe our first two or three properties were bought with money that I actually worked a job, received a paycheck for and then used to invest in real estate.

For the most part, we funded the acquisition of our real estate investments using income from our existing portfolio, sort of a snowball effect if you will. We reinvested all of our income from real estate for 12 years. Only recently have we started taking owner draws each month. As we reach 50 years old, it seemed like it was time to enjoy some of the fruits of our labor!

Important to point out, this real estate investment portfolio *is in addition to*, the traditional mutual fund and retirement account investments we made over the years. While we are heavily weighted in real estate, we also have nice retirement accounts for our golden years and 529s for the kid's college.

Now we look at the wealth we have built together over the years and are content we will be comfortable in old age and not a burden on our kids. Additionally, we should be able to pass a "generational" changing legacy on to our children. More on what that exactly means in the "Final Thoughts" chapter. College for our kids is covered. We can afford whatever school they can get into. But our journey certainly wasn't easy, there were many ups and downs along the way. Finances can be a leading cause of relationship issues.

This book is a "how-to" and certainly positively focused on real estate. But it is also a story of personal sacrifice in the near term while in anticipation of a long term gain. Before embarking on a journey similar to the one I've just described, partners must be like minded and talk about financial goals often.

We made several mistakes along the way to be sure, but definitely got it right more than we screwed up. I'll share many of the successes and failures in the coming pages! Not sure how much of our successful real estate moves were luck or good timing and how much was skill but regardless, we are very blessed and thankful.

So to answer the question posed in the title of this chapter, "Why, real estate?"…we'll I've just explained it! I am very eager to share with you in the following pages what we've learned and what has made real estate such a successful investment for our family's future.

Chapter 2: Setting the Conditions

I always get a chuckle out of these "buy real estate with no money down" seminars that roll through town from time to time. What a half-truth! Unless planning to live in the investment property, most banks will only go 75% loan to value on a conventional loan for an investment property. This means when securing a conventional mortgage from the bank, 25% down payment will be required. Banks aren't stupid! They aren't going to let an investor off the street have a 100% loan to value mortgage for an investment property that the buyer could just walk away from and leave the bank holding the bag! Bottom line, it usually takes cash on hand to invest in rental properties.

Not to worry, there are creative ways to finance rental property investments. However, it requires good planning. Before shopping for that first investment property, the conditions must be set. Building a good credit score and debt to income ratio is an important first step. It also takes capital! I already shared that my wife and I were in our mid 30's before we saved up enough money to buy our first investment property, a duplex that we occupied. Investing in real estate is a lot more than just raising the down payment and securing financing. Before calling that first real estate agent and shopping for a property there is a lot to consider. Let's dive in!

Establish Goals for the Investment

This will fundamentally drive the type of property to look for. If desiring a rental property that is likely to produce a monthly income but appreciate more slowly in value, then multi-family may be a good choice. If just looking for a safe place to invest some money beyond the stock market and monthly net income is less important, then perhaps a single family property in a good location that will appreciate more rapidly may be the best option.

In either case, it is extremely important to remember real estate is a long term investment. If needing to "cash out" the investment in five or less years, real estate is probably not the right place to tie up your capital. There are folks who have made a lot of quick money flipping real estate but flips aren't my area of expertise! Also, going back to the example in the first chapter, it's important to remember that $451 in net monthly rental income may not feel like a lot at first. Especially, when you are working your butt off to actively manage the property!

But let's say you reinvest those profits and over the course of 10 years buy four more duplexes (as we did). Factoring in regular rent increases, within a decade you've created a very nice net monthly income that should be approaching $50000 a year. Given the tax breaks in the here and now, that $50k is actually a lot better than it sounds! Not to mention, after a decade in business the portfolio of properties should be approaching a million dollars in equity. Not too shabby for a side hustle!

The first step in preparing to invest in rental properties is determine long term goals. My wife and I certainly did. Our long term goal was to invest in rental properties that produced monthly income that we could grow through reinvesting and use as the down payment to buy more properties. A snowball effect to grow our rental business. As tempting as it was, we didn't touch the income from our properties for nearly 12 years. We reinvested every penny. You may have already guessed, we are partial to multi-family because of the generally higher monthly net income, but we have also successfully invested in single family rental properties as well.

In fact, we bought the single family home we live in now with the intention of turning it into a rental some day!

How long will you use rental income to grow the business? When will you start taking owner draws? Will you dispose of the investment in 10, 20 or 30 years? Important to note, your capital is locked into the investment for that timeframe. Time, more so than anticipated profit, is the primary consideration when establishing real estate investing goals.

Only recently did we start using net income to augment our living expenses. Someday we intend to use the income as a means to early retirement. We have no definite plans to begin disposing of our properties until a need arises or we are just ready to move on from real estate. However, we are very comfortable in the fact we could use the equity to completely pay for our kids college, our primary residence mortgage, a vacation home or any combination of the three! Investment goals are important, especially when dealing with real estate. Thankfully we are achieving our goals.

Complete Initial Market Analysis

We'll talk at length about location, location, location, but before finding a property, at the macro level, one must consider the market in the area of the country where they intend to invest. If residing in a high cost of living area or an economic downturn locale, then maybe it's not the right time to take the plunge or perhaps time to conduct market analysis of a different location. Nowadays there are many "out of town" rental property investors who invest in markets that have good upside potential. As related in the first chapter, we were very fortunate to reside in two areas of the nation where quality properties were still affordable and rents remained respectable.

Wanting to own real estate is not enough, it takes some serious analysis to go from vision to reality. My wife and I were able to realize our dream of owning rental properties while I served in the military. Finding a good market to invest in didn't happen completely by accident as my story in chapter one may have implied. Our opportunities to invest were the culmination of initial market research, planning and yes, a little luck. There are several Army postings inside and outside the United States where it would have been near impossible for us to realize our goal of investing in real estate. So early on, while still stationed in New York, where we definitely were not able to invest, I began diligently researching Army bases that had favorable real estate markets nearby.

Fort Hood, Texas came up at the top of the list. Central Texas has a lot to offer and in the early 2000s the area was experiencing a real estate boom. Prices were good and as I mentioned briefly in the last chapter, Killeen, TX zones somewhat uniquely in that the city allows multi-family homes mixed in with predominantly single family neighborhoods.

So as we left New York in 2007 to attend a required Army one year school in Fort Leavenworth, Kansas, we made a decision to start shaping our follow on assignment to land at Fort Hood, TX. Fortunately, we were able to influence the Army process and get orders for Texas! Before graduating from the training course in 2008, we had already traveled to Killeen, picked out a duplex and closed on the home. We purchased two more duplexes during our nearly four year assignment to Fort Hood. Our three duplexes in Texas are proven performers and their values have increased tremendously since we've owned them.

My wife and I successfully did a macro level analysis before beginning our journey in real estate investing. Was this more luck than skill? Maybe, but as the old saying goes you make your own luck. We started researching nearly two years early to determine the Army post most conducive to real estate investing. If we hadn't started early, acted decisively and shaped the process, we could have ended up anywhere and may not have been able to start our real estate journey. Ironically, we landed in our second market, Huntsville, AL quite by accident. Fortunately, Huntsville had many of the same real estate investment opportunities that central Texas offered.

Deciding to pick up and move or invest in a city far from home is a substantial but important step in setting the conditions. Maybe the area you live in now just isn't the place or maybe it's perfect. Performing a very top level market analysis to check key demographics such as average home prices, rents, incomes and job opportunities is critical to determine what part of the nation in which to invest. Once you've determined which market you want to invest in, then comes the detailed planning!

Get Financing Set and Ready

Even in the mid-2000s when we started investing in real estate, if a good deal presented itself, you had to be ready to move quickly. Today, in the red hot real estate market it is even more competitive. In our current area, homes often stay on the market for only a number of hours. It is absolutely critical to have a pre-qualification letter and / or proof of funds before beginning a search for an investment.

Conventional mortgages for investment properties will have slightly higher interest rates than a loan for an owner occupied property. Makes sense, the bank is just covering its interest. It is a lot easier for someone to walk away from an investment property than their own home! As already stated, unless the owner intends to occupy the property expect about a max 75% loan-to-value for a conventional mortgage on a pure investment property. Additionally, conventional mortgages will only work for one to four unit investment properties. Anything over a four unit structure (quadraplex) and a business loan will be required. Generally speaking, business loan terms are a little tougher for the individual investor and can include some rigid stipulations to include a balloon payment after 5-7 years.

So what's the good news? If you have good credit and are disciplined, there are creative ways to finance properties at reasonable interest rates that can increase the profitability of an investment. First, low or no money down loans are great for owner occupied properties. Qualifying individuals can use VA, FHA and other government secured loans for investment properties if the buyer resides in the property. These loans require little to no money down and usually banks will offer more attractive interest rates for government backed loans.

If the owner moves out of the home, not to worry, the mortgage remains in place at the great interest rate! Important to remember, the less down payment, the more the monthly mortgage which cuts into net monthly income on a rental property. For a first time investor, a government backed loan for an owner occupied duplex is definitely the best way to get into real estate investing with minimum required capital.

A more creative way to finance a real estate purchase may be to borrow money using investment accounts or retirement accounts as collateral. Can't stress enough that this takes incredible discipline since failing to pay back the loan will result in forfeiting a large part of retirement or investment savings, sometimes with additional penalties. That being said, interest rates for these types of loans are usually decent and in some cases, such as with the government employee's Thrift Savings Plan (TSP), the interest rate is outstanding. Be sure to read the fine print before entering into one of these loans as there may be restrictions on what the loans can be used for.

Going this route will usually require some out of pocket capital to make up the complete purchase price, but on a positive note, the property will be owned outright as there won't be a mortgage lien against the property. Additionally, these types of loans often won't show up on a credit report.

We purchased a small single family condo that was distressed for $36k using a $40k loan from our TSP account to pay the purchase price and needed repairs. Although we didn't make any profit on this property initially, the rental income was enough to pay back the loan in just a few years. Also in that time, the value of the property nearly doubled! The funds used from our TSP loan had yielded a much higher rate of return than if we had left it sitting in the retirement account! We made a similar profitable property purchase a couple of years later by using a loan with our taxable investment account as collateral. Of course, when offering up an investment account as collateral, the funds can't be accessed so be sure to have a plan!

Still another creative way to finance investment properties is the use of credit card or personal loans. This is absolutely a risky venture and takes incredible discipline. If you have good credit and receive those special 0% courtesy check offers for periods of 18 months or greater, then this might be an option.

It is imperative to pay off credit card loans during the 0% introductory period as the interest rates afterwards are enormous. Additionally, these types of loans will most definitely appear on a credit report as revolving debt which could negatively impact the investor's credit score. Also, read the fine print as there are sometimes limitations on what credit card or personal loans can be spent on. I just can't stress enough, these types of loans present incredible risk, be sure to consider every angle before pursuing this option.

We purchased a small single family condo using a $25k, 0% credit card loan for 18 months along with $25k cash from our taxable investment account. Although the rental income didn't completely cover the $1400 each month required to pay off the credit card loan, we used income from our other properties to make up the difference. We paid off the credit card loan using rental income during the 18 month introductory period. The property is a proven performer and like our other homes is steadily increasing in value. Most significantly we own it outright, 100% equity!

The bottom line is getting financing together prior to purchase is an absolutely critical step to real estate investing. Securing a conventional loan with crappy terms or worse yet getting sideways on a creative finance arrangement can not only make real estate investment not profitable, but potentially financially ruinous. Do the homework and maintain a good understanding of all the financing options.

Find the Yes

How often have we heard "no" from a loan application, job interview or any other request and just walked away. Perhaps even more relatable, how many times have we heard "yes" but not necessarily on the terms we were hoping for but just accepted it? Unfortunately, there are a lot of "no's" when getting started in real estate investing. Whether it is a seller declining an offer or a bank rejecting a loan application, the real estate investor must be able to find a yes to get their business off the ground. After a "no", perform an analysis as to what is causing the less than favorable response and correct the issue or in some cases go in a different direction, but above all never stop fighting. The real estate investor, can't give up when they hear "no".

Getting to yes is easier said than done. Oftentimes we've put a lot of effort into our proposal, done all of our homework and have the best laid plan for starting a real estate investing journey. When we hear no, we may feel completely defeated, it is perfectly normal to want to give up. But consider the other persons perspective, "no" is a lot easier than "yes". There is less risk and no is always the safe bet. More often than not, we all default to "no" unless we have compelling evidence on why we should say yes.

Which brings us to the essence of getting to yes. First, ensure there is a clear understanding of the root cause for the negative response, then make required changes. Did the seller reject your offer? Relook your cap rate analysis and see if there is room to maneuver. For formal considerations such as a loan application, the lender will usually spell out reasons for disapproval. While the reasons may be challenging to overcome, such as a low credit score, the remedy is clear, improve the credit score. Commit to developing and executing a course of action to implement a fix. It may take some time, but do what it takes *now* to overcome what is causing the no.

Still another option is to go find a yes. Using the loan example, more likely than not, the next lender will probably still be a no. That being said, it is always prudent to get a second opinion when encountering a no. Every lender conducts operations a little differently and follows differing business practices.

After our fourth mortgage for an investment property, we encountered an issue with our preferred lender while trying to acquire a fifth loan for another duplex opportunity. Due to certain regulatory guidance, this particular lender could not approve an individual for more than four mortgages. Our dreams of building a real estate empire were over! Not so fast. After calling around, I learned not all lenders follow the same regulatory guidance. One bank responded, "we will approve as many loans as you qualify for"! We established a relationship with this bank and haven't looked back. Just this year, we completed four refinances with them. If I had given up on the first no, we wouldn't have pursued our last four duplexes and our net worth wouldn't be near where it is now!

Determine Acceptable Risk and Make a Commitment

Risk from investing in real estate is usually thought of as purchasing a property that either does not produce any income or appreciate in value at an acceptable rate. I am firmly convinced, in most areas of the nation, the likely hood of this occurring is fairly low. Real estate is overall just a safer bet. While risk is the correct word, let's use the word sacrifice for a moment. I've already touched on this while sharing our journey. Investing in real estate, requires personal sacrifice and a level of deprivation which are not present in other investment products. While it takes near term sacrifice for any worker to save and invest money on a tight budget, real estate investing requires the additional sacrifice of time. Losing time is just as much of a risk as losing money. After all time *is* money, to use the old expression. But first let's take a look at the financial risk.

I've already mentioned that my wife and I were raised to live below our means. We clearly delineate between needs and wants before every purchase. This is critical to raising that initial capital for investing in a property and to fight the urge to take an owner draw when the rental starts netting a profit each month. Simply put, real estate investing requires depriving oneself of unnecessary wants. There may be times when a real estate investor may feel "poor" but actually have several hundred thousand or millions in equity! The equity in real estate is a long term investment and certainly not liquid. It cannot be tapped easily. In the near term (think 20 years) real estate investing will most likely not lead to an exotic sports car or lavish lifestyle.

That is why the risks to personal finances when tying up capital in real estate must be weighed and considered carefully. If with a partner, this absolutely must be a mutual decision. It has been tough for us at points over the years. We could have used the money we sunk into real estate or our rental profits to buy a bigger house, better car, nicer smart phone or just about anything. But instead, we kept our capital tied up in real estate and sunk our monthly net gains back into more properties. Never underestimate the gravity of this psychological challenge. Once invested in real estate, capital is tied up for several years!

Of course the payoff occurs down the road and usually comes in the form of early retirement, kid's college paid for and debt free living. But we as humans are sometimes terribly short sighted. I can't stress enough review and acknowledge the risk (or sacrifice) to personal finances that investing in real estate requires. It is somewhat difficult to undo once you've made the plunge.

The other risk (or sacrifice) is the time a real estate investment will consume. Unlike putting 10% of a paycheck into a retirement account, investing and actively managing real estate requires giving up personal time. We will go into detail in the coming chapters, but just expect that plumbing, air conditioners and the 100s of other things that can go wrong will go wrong on a Saturday night. If not on a Saturday night, a Tuesday night after a long day's work at the day job. There is just never a good time.

Actively managing rental properties absolutely means giving up free time to tend to the investment. I will provide numerous examples of where rental properties have been a real suck on my free time. This came at the expense of my family; this is the definition of sacrifice. Will the juice be worth the squeeze?

Lastly, buying and renting property to others is inherently a people business in so many ways. There are ways to reduce it, but at the end of the day finding, buying and managing rentals takes near constant human interaction. Anytime people are involved in an operation, risk is introduced. I am talking all sorts of risk, much of which we will go into greater detail later in the book. If the "people" risk seems unacceptable, then perhaps stick to the retirement accounts or taxable mutual funds!

The word commitment is thrown around a lot but it is certainly applicable in real estate investing more so than squirreling away funds in a retirement account. This is probably a big reason why not everyone invests in real estate! Discuss with your partner, determine how much risk you are willing to take and make the commitment together. Real estate is not something to be ventured into unknowingly.

Establish Core Values and Business Practices

There's really not a good chapter to put this section in but I want to include it upfront to set the tone for the rest of the book. When we first started owning and managing rental properties, many of my friends would jokingly refer to me as "slumlord". Although I knew they were using the term in complete jest, it still stung a little bit. "Rent collector" has had a generally negative connotation since biblical times and with good reason. Most of us have experienced greedy landlords who could care less about the tenant and were clearly only focused on making a buck. Whether investing in one duplex or a 100 unit apartment complex, it is important to establish the values for your rental property business.

It always irks me a bit when hearing real estate investors' gloss over the human element of the investment. It really boils down to the golden rule, do unto others as you'd have them do unto you. Most of us have paid rent at one point in our lives but many investors seem to forget what it was like. The very act of paying seemingly exorbitant rates for a basic life necessity, shelter, is not the most pleasant experience for a tenant. Tenants will know at first glance if a property owner is looking to make a buck or is really committed to making renting as pleasant as possible. As we'll cover later in the "establishing a relationship" chapter, tenants will mirror back the values and behaviors they encounter. There are a few core values and operating principles we follow in our rental business. I'd like to think we wouldn't depart from these core values if we went from 17 to 200 rental units.

We are service providers. Our business is to provide clean, well maintained and safe homes for our tenants. My wife does most of the customer facing interaction in our business and I handle the repairs. I usually don't share with tenants that I am the owner until it comes up in conversation, sometimes while I am under their sink or wedged behind their toilet. You can visibly see the appreciation in their eyes to know not only do the owners rapidly respond to their maintenance request, but also is personally fixing their problem.

Rent a little below market. Next chapter we'll talk about accounting for vacancies when determining the cap rate for a property. When offering properties slightly below market rent, vacancies usually becomes a non-issue as most tenants are looking for the best value. More importantly, especially in today's red hot market, tenants will recognize immediately you are not a landlord intent on gouging rent. Tenants recognize greed and will respond accordingly. It is a real pleasure when we are thanked for not gouging rent like everyone else.

Modest rent increases every two years. By modest I mean in the $50 range. A $20 or $30 per month increase may seem small, but is a big jump for someone who is struggling to meet their monthly financial commitments. While sometimes it may be necessary to increase rent in subsequent years, we try our best not to. Unfortunately, we see a lot of fellow landlords jacking rent up $100 or $200 per month upon lease renewal every year. Just recently we took on a new tenant who shared that the rent at her previous residence went up $400 so she left (and came to us). In our humble opinion, gouging rent is taking a short term gain but a long term loss.

People first. Renting property is a people business and people must come first. Not only is discriminating against tenants based on sex, religion or race just plain wrong, it is illegal. We assess tenants based on the strength of their application from our tenant screening service. Purely quantitative. But what if there is a rare instance when two prospective tenants come back identically qualified? One is a single parent with two kids looking to rent the home because it is zoned for better schools while the other is a single person who just wants the extra bedrooms for storage and a home office. In these situations, its best to talk to people. What we've found is most folks understand and rather see the single parent provide a good home for their children. While we assess prospective tenants via numbers, we never forget people first.

Clean and modern. When I used to rent it was always the little features in a home that jumped out at me. Good solid blinds that actually block the light, ceiling fan for that upstairs room that is hard to cool, a refrigerator with an ice maker and fixtures / furnishings that don't look like they are from the 1970s. It has always irked me when I see a rental property with the absolute cheapest materials, be it blinds, appliances or fixtures. Good 2" blinds are only a few dollars more, modern appliances maybe more expensive but the tenant will appreciate them so much. These investments are important and I daresay payoff in the long run. Similarly, when a prospective tenant views one of our properties, the residence will be nearly spotless. As service providers, we feel this is what we owe them. Likewise we want to send a message about our expectations on how the tenant should maintain the residence!

These are just a few of our guiding practices. I really don't see us departing from them. Establishing values and business practices are personal decisions but they must be considered before diving into investing. Some of the practices I mentioned above may cut into an investor's bottom line in the near term but I assure you it won't break the bank and will pay off in the long run. Real estate is a winning proposition! Furthermore, the personal satisfaction of being fair, honest and not greedy is worth so much more than a couple hundred extra bucks every month.

At times in this book it may sound like I am trying to talk the reader out of investing in real estate. Nothing could be farther from the truth! Know that I am a former career Soldier. One of our many attributes (some may call it a fault) is that we are realists. With a degree of preparation and action, most challenges can be overcome. Those challenges that upon a realistic review, are unsurmountable, must be bypassed or otherwise avoided. It is simply how my realist brain is programed to think and how I'll share my thoughts in this book. You will see a lot of real talk in the chapters that follow!

We've had outstanding success with real estate investing but it is because my wife and I viewed the task through a realist's lens. Do we dream? Of course, but in the real world, there is not a lot of time for speculation. Investing is in simplest terms a math problem. That is my issue with some of the real estate investment strategies. High on ideals but low on reality. The math has to work. After we established realistic goals, secured financing, made the commitment and set our values, we were ready to make our fortunes on real estate.

You maybe thinking, this is all well and good, but honestly, how does the average worker, just trying to make ends meet, build enough capital to start a rental property side business? Glad you asked! In my book, *"Millionaire on a Worker's Budget: Five Financial Truths to Build Wealth"* I suggest there are five financial truths the average worker must espouse in their daily lives to earn a million dollar net worth in a reasonable amount of time, about 20-25 years. These truths all work together to enable the average worker to build that capital for their first real estate purchase.

Truth #1: Invest Early, Invest Often
To build wealth, saving must be a priority over a lifetime. This inevitably means giving up access to hard earned income during the here and now for use later in life. The time value of compounding money can never be underestimated. To be a millionaire on a worker's budget you must save aggressively your entire working life.

Truth #2: Be Frugal
To become a millionaire on a worker's budget, one must spend conservatively. This all comes down to understanding needs versus wants and showing self-control in *every purchase and financial move*. This is probably the hardest truth as it takes an incredible amount of patience, discipline and sacrifice.

Truth #3: Collect Rent, Don't Pay It

I stated this truth in the opening paragraph of this book and I can't stress it enough. It will be challenging for a worker to build a million dollar net worth in their forties or fifties if paying rent their whole adult life. Moreover, real estate should be an important part of every investment portfolio. The benefits of real estate investing is no secret. But make no mistake, owning real estate is more than just an investment, it is a bona fide part time job!

Truth #4: Be Diligent

This is more than just working double shifts and putting in overtime; just about everyone works hard. To become a millionaire as a worker, diligence is a truth that must become a life value. This means when something is broke, fix it…now. Never walk past a wrong, take immediate action. Get to yes or move on. These behaviors will make incredible impacts in all aspects of life, especially in one's ability to earn and build wealth.

Truth #5: Knowledge is Money

There are really two kinds of knowledge when related to finance. First, the knowledge gained through a commitment to lifelong self-study in order to make informed decisions. From the most basic daily purchases to which investment products are best, every single financial decision requires gaining knowledge and developing understanding. Second, is knowledge in the more traditional sense, formal education and training. Without a degree or a certified skill, a worker will have a hard time increasing earning potential over the years.

There are certainly many strategies for building wealth. These are the truths that enabled my wife and I to build our portfolio of properties and become financially comfortable before our 50s. Important to point out, I've spent 16 pages talking about setting the conditions before even beginning to talk about looking for that first property! Setting the conditions is a critical first step and may take years. Once the conditions are set, it's time to take the plunge into real estate. Read on to learn how to select the best property and stop paying rent!

Chapter 3: Selecting the Best Property

An old adage says that money is made from real estate when it is purchased. I believe this is a truth on many levels. First and foremost, the math has to work on a property to make it a profitable investment. Pay too much and the math may never work! For the math to work, there are many different variables that must be considered before making an offer, going under contract and closing on your first investment property.

To Use a Buyer's Agent or Not

When ready to shop for that first investment property, the investor may consider securing a buyer's real estate agent to assist in the search. Whether to use a buyer's agent or not is truly a matter of personal preference, but I am certainly happy to offer my thoughts on the subject!

Bottom line, unless I am searching for an investment property far from our current location, I don't use a buyer's agent. Like many topics in this book, I formed this perspective through experiences, mostly bad. Quick disclaimer before sharing my thoughts, I mean no disrespect to real estate agents. There are some absolutely amazing folks working in the real estate profession. I respect the profession and have several friends who are real estate agents. Heck, I am considering getting my license someday!

Many folks, mostly real estate agents, would recommend using a buyer's agent when searching for a property but I don't and there are several reasons why. First, I've found very few real estate agents are familiar with rental properties and especially multi-family. I've found some that may not set up their search tools appropriately and don't find opportunities any better than I can on a home finder website. Often, I identified a multi-family opportunity before my buyer's agent!

Additionally, a rental property investor needs to ask countless questions and know many facts about the investment property under consideration before making an offer. When it comes to multifamily, I've just found that many buyer's agents have trouble either understanding the question or providing complete answers. Important to remember, most often buyer's agents are helping clients through more of an emotional decision about the purchase of a personal residence rather than helping a client close on a business deal.

Second, and this sounds horrible, oftentimes the buyer's agent is not very motivated to return your calls and find answers to your questions when considering a $250k duplex. They obviously had rather spend their time on the client looking for a $500k or higher personal residence. I would submit that an investment purchase is a much more complex deal than a personal residence. Unfortunately, an investment property deal will suck up more of the agent's time yet potentially yield less commission. Important to remember, I am not talking about every real estate agent! There are some really motivated folks out there who truly love helping clients with a purchase. But there are several who just may not be motivated to put in the work an investment requires.

Lastly, and this is the most important, when going directly to the seller's agent, the buyer gains leverage when negotiating. When using just a seller's agent, the agent gets to keep the entire 5-6% commission! Oftentimes to close a deal, the seller's agent may agree to give the seller back a point or two of their commission. This could be the motivation a seller needs to get under contract! This is the definition of a win-win.

Not to mention the time saved in this red hot real estate market during negotiations by cutting out an extra layer.

Real estate agents will be emphatic that a buyer needs an agent to protect their interests but I am not convinced. The contracts are not that complicated and the seller's agent can answer questions just as easily. We maintain a positive world view and think there are very few seller's agents who would jeopardize their livelihood and reputation to swindle or deceive a buyer. Every time we've went directly to the seller's agent, we have had positive experiences. But again, whether to use a buyer's agent when searching for an investment is truly a question of personal preference. Obviously, if you are looking for an investment property three states over, a buyer's agent is almost a necessity. Find a good buyer's agent you can trust if it's the right fit for you.

Location, Location, Location

The primary and most notable factor in real estate investing is of course, location, location, location. I know its clichéd but it is absolutely true. If money is made from real estate when the asset is acquired, then no single factor is more important than where the property is located. We talked briefly about market analysis at the macro level last chapter or more simply put, determining the regional market in which to invest. After the market is determined, at the micro level, there are many more considerations about location. Fortunately, the same factors that drive up home prices are what impacts rental markets.

Choosing an investment property is certainly a case where cheaper is not always better. Cheap properties will result in cheap rent and more than likely will lead to more headaches than the amateur investor wants to deal with. Ideally, finding a multi-family property that is not located in a high density multi-family area, but rather mixed in among single family homes is perfect.

Many cities tend to keep multi-family dwellings zoned separately from single family homes. We were fortunate that our first duplex was a new construction set on a street with other duplexes within a community of predominantly neat little brick single family homes.

Finding a city such as Killeen, TX that zones in this manner is unique but there are some. Regardless, if a multi-family property is sitting in an undesirable part of town, it will be very slow to increase in value or rents. Look for a multi-family located adjacent to or just at the edge of desirable single family neighborhoods.

One of the biggest factors that determines rents and purchase price is schools. Single or multifamily homes zoned for well rated public schools will increase in value and pull more rent. School zoning is the first thing we look at when purchasing a property.

We are always wary of fixer uppers, but an ugly duckling at the right price in an amazing location may be worth the gamble. Our second duplex was a bank owned property and had been vacant for over a year. The worst thing that can happen to a home is to set empty! It sat in a great neighborhood with good schools within walking distance so we made a low ball offer and surprisingly the bank accepted. Took a week off from work and 10 hour days fixing it up but we've kept that property rented ever since and it has almost doubled in value! If going the fixer upper route, developing some do it yourself skills is imperative or margins will quickly shrink.

A few years later we completed a similar deal in Huntsville, AL on a small condo unit that was distressed but in a good location. It took a while to close but we ended up only paying $36000 for the property! After spending about

$6000 to update, we rented the property right away and it has nearly tripled in value. I don't always recommend fixer uppers, but if they are located in a good area it's worth a consideration. One note, when assessing a property and upon initial inspection determining it needs $5000 of repairs...add another $5000 for items that are lurking just under the surface! Bottom line, consider location first, then search for those potential fixer upper deals.

There are several other factors to choosing a good location for investment properties that are mostly common sense. Multi-families located in rural areas with long commutes to employment, restaurants, grocery and retail may be harder to rent. That doesn't mean all rural areas are bad investments as it really depends on the type of property.

A one bedroom / one bath duplex apartment in a rural setting will have a very small market of potential renters. Younger, single people usually wouldn't be interested in this type of home as it is farther away from work and entertainment. Perhaps a single, retired person would be interested in renting a one bedroom in a rural setting. But how many single, retired people are looking for apartments at any given time? The exact same one bed / one bath apartment in the middle of a city may demand high rent and have a waiting list of prospective tenants!

On the other hand, a three bedroom, two bath in a rural setting that is a reasonable commute to the city but also zoned for good county schools may rent very quickly. Many families want to take advantage of the county school system and get their kids out of an urban area. Some single folks may look to take on some roommates in order to save money and would be willing to extend their commute by moving a little further out of town. The point is, consider the market for prospective tenants based on the location and type of home.

This is good old fashioned detailed market analysis and must be completed before the purchase. Fortunately, analyzing rental markets is mostly common sense and there are tools available to help. There are a lot of good apartment finder web sites that can be used to find comparable rents in the area to determine rental potential. Additionally, there are many web sites that will provide investors with demographic data to include income, family size, crime rates and age for a particular area. With just a few quick internet searches, it is easy to determine if a particular area has a high density of families, retirees or single workers. Based on the demographics, one can determine what types of property will be most desirable for renters.

The bottom line of all this is location, location, location determines rent, rent, rent which once you factor in the various expenses reveals how valuable an investment property will be.

Determine Capitalization Rate for a Potential Property

Capitalization or Cap rate as it is often called is simply the net income (rent after subtracting all expenses) divided by the value of the asset and expressed as a percentage. For instance, if annual net rental income for a property is $10000 and the property is valued at $100000 then the cap rate is 10%. This is the "math" used when looking for a property to determine if the investment is right for you. Generally speaking, an investor wants to be in the 8-10% cap rate range to make a good deal for a real estate investment.

Before diving into a more formal method for calculating cap rate, I'll share what I call the "field expedient" method for determining if a property is even close to a good asking price. Field expedient is an old Army term for throwing together a solution on the fly! I like to call it the 10%

rule. Let's say you are relaxing at home and surfing your favorite on line real estate site looking for the next great multi-family investment opportunity. There is a good looking duplex for sale and the seller is asking $400000. Take 10% of the ask ($40000) and divide by 12. This equals $3333 per month estimated gross for the property or almost $1700 per unit.

If you've done an initial market research for the area and know that there is no possible way that class of property at that location will bring over $1200 per unit given the current rental market conditions, then the sellers ask is too high. May be best to keep on scrolling or be prepared to do some negotiating!

Using the reverse of the 10% rule, one can figure out a good price range to start a search. If $1200 per month per unit is the average rent for a good duplex in the area, then take $2400 and multiply by 12. This equals $28800. Multiply by 10 and you get $288000. This would be a good starting point

Field Expediant Cap Rate or the 10% rule					
Based on Seller's Ask					
Seller's Ask	Divide by 12 months	Divide by 10	Divide by 2 (for duplex)	
400000	33333	3333	1667	Max possible rent
Based on Local Rents					
Max Market Rent for Type of Property	Multiply by 12 months	Multiply by 10	Multiply by 2 (for duplex)	
1200	14400	144000	288000	Optimal Purchase Price

for a search. If you scroll down from the $400000 property and see one listed for $300000 it's probably worth pausing and looking at the ad closer. I can't stress enough the "10% rule" is just an initial screening tool to get an investor in the ball park. There is no real science behind it. A detailed capitalization rate analysis must be performed before even thinking about making an offer!

There are numerous ways to more formally calculate cap rate and I recommend figuring it conservatively by using maximum projected expenses and minimum expected rents. I am by no means an Excel expert, but using a spreadsheet with very simple formulas is probably the best way to do the math. Let's walk through a cap rate analysis I performed on a property a few years back to get a feel for the numbers.

The following capitalization rate analysis was actually performed for a five unit multi-family we were considering in a low rent area of town. Starting from the top you can see I figured cap rate based on anticipated rents per each unit (three of the units included an extra bedroom, thus higher rent). Again, I always go conservative so these numbers are a little below actual market.

Cap Rate Worksheet for 1801 Any St.				
Subject Property: 5 units (2X1BR, 3X2BR)				
Monthly Rent	725 / 600	700 / 575	675 / 550	650 / 525
Gross Annual	40500	39000	37500	36000
10%vacancy	-4050	-3900	-3750	-3600
Property Taxes	-2613	-2613	-2613	-2613
Insurance	-1200	-1200	-1200	-1200
Solid Waste	0	0	0	0
Pest Control	0	0	0	0
Lawn	0	0	0	0
Utilities	0	0	0	0
Cleaning / Maint	-230	-230	-230	-230
Repairs	-3303	-3303	-3303	-3303
Net Operating Income	29104	27754	26404	25054
10%	291040	277540	264040	250540
9.50%	306358	292147	277937	263726
9.00%	323378	308378	293378	278378
8.50%	342400	326518	310635	294753
8.00%	363800	346925	330050	313175
7.50%	388053	370053	352053	334053
7%	415771	396486	377200	357914
Average	347257	331150	315042	298934
P/I (30yr/4.5%) 150k	760	760	760	760
P/I Annual	9120	9120	9120	9120
Annual Income	19984	18634	17284	15934

Next we figure our expenses. Note I included a 10% vacancy rate. In 14 years in the rental property business, I've never had close to a 10% vacancy rate, especially in today's red hot rental market. But again, I can't stress enough, plan conservatively so you've got a good idea of the potential risks!

Other expenses will include property taxes, insurance, any utilities you may plan on including and Homeowners Association (HOA) fees as applicable as well as maintenance. Notice there are zeros for many of the expenses. These are items I planned to do myself! We have a whole chapter on maintenance and DIY coming up. Also include a line for "repairs" which is different than maintenance. Upon inspection, you may determine a property will need HVAC, a roof and new windows within the next 10 years. When figuring cap rate, you can usually spread these costs out over a few years.

Once all expenses are considered, subtract the total from the gross annual income which gives the Net Operating Income (NOI). Now take the NOI and divide it by the price of the property. In the example above, I've taken the NOI and calculated it for a range of purchase prices from 7%-10% capitalization rate as well as made the calculations for varying potential rents.

Now comes the most important part, analyze the data. Using the spreadsheet above, we can see that if the property grossed $3375 per month in rents a purchase price in the 8%-10% cap rate range should be $364000 to $291000. Obviously higher cap rate is better. Let's say the seller is asking $400000 for the property, they are pretty high according to our cap rate determination. Consider going in with a lower offer and negotiating. If the seller won't budge, don't be afraid to move on to the next opportunity! But let's say the seller is asking $350k for the property.

Because we've set the conditions by having a pre-qual letter from the bank and enough capital for a substantial down payment, we can make an offer of $310000 for the property. Assuming the seller accepts, with closing costs our basis for the property will be around $320000 which as we see on the worksheet will yield about a 9% cap rate. Not too shabby of a deal!

But wait, we aren't done yet! Note I didn't figure mortgage principle and interest as part of the net operating expenses. Some investors do but many don't when figuring cap rate. I usually do figure in mortgage principle and interest as operating expenses but for this particular example I chose not to. I don't recall exactly what I had lined up for this particular property but looks like I was planning on getting a 30 year, $150000 loan at 4.5% interest. Once P&I is subtracted from the NOI that would leave almost $20000 per year in "take home" or net profit. Add in the tax advantages and the $20000 feels a lot more like $25000. Pretty good for one building! Additionally, don't forget the value of the property will appreciate thus building equity.

All that being said, we passed on this particular property. It was older and the nuances of managing a five unit property in a lower rent part of town is a lot different than the duplexes and condos we are currently invested in. It came down to sticking with what we know and our personal tolerance for risk.

This is case in point, when considering a property, determining cap rate goes hand in hand with location, location, location. Once you've found the location, completed the math, made that offer and gone under contract, there is one more critical step before closing on your first property. Have the property professionally inspected!

Have the Property Professionally Inspected

Most of us have the basic know how and common sense to recognize the big items when considering an investment property for purchase. If the home is 20 years old and has the original roof, then it will likely need a roof within the next 5-10 years. Roofs can cost from $5k - $30k depending on whether filing an insurance claim or paying out of pocket. If the water heater has visible rust or is over 10-15 years old, there is another $1000. Windows original? Looking at $6000-$20000 within the next 10 years. HVAC over 10 years? Tack on another $5k. Flooring, paint, cabinets, or appliances look shoddy? Easy fixes, but those are bills that add up in the thousands. You get the point.

Obviously if all these things are in immediate need of replacement, then you are looking at a "rehab" or "fixer upper". Repairs will need to be made before a tenant can move in and as stated previously, it is probably more headache than the average investor wants to deal with. In most cases, I'd recommend walking away unless the location is so great and purchase price so low it would be worth the time, money and hassle to make all those repairs.

But let's say an investor comes across that 20 year old duplex and the owner has managed it well. It has new paint, carpet, appliances and the roof was replaced within the last three years. Water heater is new and the windows while original, are of high quality and well maintained. One of two HVAC units have been replaced within the last three years and the home has good curb appeal.

If the math works, sounds like it is time to make an offer! Assuming your offer is accepted, there is one more critical step before closing and making the property your own. Most sales contracts include a 10 day inspection period where the buyer can have the property inspected by a licensed professional home inspector. In today's red hot real estate market, it is becoming somewhat common for buyers to waive the inspection period.

I can't imagine a more ill-conceived idea! Always, always, always have the home professionally inspected. While most of us can readily identify the big, obvious issues in a home, a licensed inspector will find the little things that can become big problems later down the road. Don't be afraid to walk out on a contract if the inspector comes back with a long list of deficiencies that the seller is unwilling to fix.

We had to walk away from a deal for a single family home that we intended to live in. The home had beautiful upgrades as we learned the owner was a skilled craftsman and did the work himself. The only problem, there were no permits for the updates and several were not within local building code. If we didn't perform a thorough home inspection, we may not have been able to secure financing or worse yet entered into a potential money pit trying to bring the property up to code!

Let me provide an example of how skipping a home inspection can cost a fortune in the long run. In early 2017 we purchased a nice two bedroom / two bath condo in our town at a great price. Just two years later, the unit had a massive water leak that could have been easily prevented. A water supply line from the kitchen sink valve to the dishwasher popped loose leaking water at 50psi pressure for a number of hours resulting in significant water damage to our condo unit and the two units below. Here is the rest of the story….

This was our seventh real estate investment property and I thought I was a master investor! This condo was pretty small and I thought I knew enough about home inspections to forego paying a licensed inspector $350 to check out all aspects of the home. Important to point out, when hiring an inspector, ensure you get a copy of their check list and if they will let you, shadow them during the inspection. You'll find the inspections they make while important, are not that difficult. Because I had seen home inspections performed at least half a dozen times in the past, I thought I could do it myself.

During my do-it-myself pre-closing inspection, I noted some of the plumbing looked outdated and questionable.

Especially the dishwasher supply line which was simply plastic tubing held onto the valve by a compression fitting. But to be truthful, I really didn't know what that meant. Come to find out, this is not up to current plumbing code as most water supplies under pressure require a hammer arrestor at the valve and a steel braided or otherwise more heavy duty supply line. An inspector would have included this in their report as a major deficiency.

Of course, I was excited to close on the deal and walked right past the problem. It cost me dearly. Would I have made repairs to this item if discovered and reported by a licensed inspector? I think so. Psychologically, there is just something about a deficiency in an official report that makes it more noteworthy. I was too focused on closing the deal and getting a tenant into the residence instead of being diligent and fixing problems.

The fallout from this leak episode took over two months to fully remediate. We came out of pocket $4000 to keep the peace with our neighbors. Working with our insurance company was a near daily battle but fortunately I was able to turn lemons into lemonade with the settlement and install a very nice, new kitchen on the cheap. That was most likely luck and timing than skill. I just happened to catch the materials on sale at the big box and was able to sub contract the repairs myself.

More impactful was the incredible stress placed on my family as well as our tenant during those two months. Thankfully, our tenant was very understanding when she and her children had to move out for a few weeks while we made repairs. She did not have a renter's insurance policy and was not compensated for some of her damaged personal items. She was very pleased with the new kitchen when she returned to the home.

This leak episode also played out at the exact time I was transitioning from my career in the Army. On a positive note, I wasn't exactly taxed with duties in my day job as I was out processing from service. If this had occurred while my career was in full swing, I don't know how I would have handled it! On the downside, I spent numerous hours each day dealing with cleaning up a rental property mess instead of focusing on transitioning to a new chapter in my life. Additionally, our family had planned a big vacation overseas with extended family to celebrate retiring from 24 years of military service. Unfortunately, I was dealing with insurance adjusters and contractors while 5000 miles from home and in a different time zone at the expense of my family.

I learned my lesson! I'll never purchase another property without a professional inspection. Home inspections are not terribly expensive, usually $300 to $500. Money well spent. More importantly, I'll never walk past a problem as little leaks can turn into nightmares costing time and thousands of dollars.

To Build or Buy

We recently completed our first build of an investment property. It wasn't the most pleasant of experiences. Since we've only built one property and didn't have the best outcome, I am not in a good position to opine as to whether building new or buying existing investment properties is better. Like most things in life it depends. There are some obvious advantages to building new, first and foremost the much lower maintenance and repair costs. But there are some hidden risks. I am happy to share our experience with building an investment property in the hopes that it could help inform an aspiring real estate investor's decision making process.

A few years ago we bought a duplex which included a quarter acre vacant lot. We purchased the place at a great price and it is performing well on the rental market. In spring of 2019 we started talking to builders about constructing a near identical duplex on the vacant quarter acre lot. An agonizing two-and-a-half years later, the project was complete...

Home builders provide cost per square foot as a rough estimate on the construction. As we spoke to different builders, the costs were coming back nearly $50 per square foot over what we were targeting. What I found is most custom builders really don't want to fool around with a ~$250K duplex made of contractor grade materials. They had much rather spend their time on the $600K+ custom homes. I understand their point of view.

About to give up on our plans, we came across a company who specialized in building on your own land and gave them a call. When I inquired about construction costs the response was they did not build any homes over $80 per square foot. They had me at hello! The company used our existing duplex to draw up the blueprints for our new construction. We secured new construction financing and in November of 2019, we went under contract with the builder.

The initial planning and design phase went pretty smooth but when it came to execution the schedule quickly went off the rails. Scheduling a competent surveyor and a geologist to lay out the build and septic plan proved challenging. It was mid 2020 before we could even get the required permits from the county for the build.

A global pandemic in early 2020 also certainly didn't help things. Thankfully, many of the materials were procured before prices skyrocketed. The foundation was finally poured in August 2020. At points during the construction, progress would move very rapidly. For instance framing and roofing was completed in a week. Then the structure would sit. And sit. Untouched for months. The superintendents assigned to this construction were nice but very young and inexperienced. After about a year and a half of delays, the CEO of the company eventually took oversight of the project personally which helped push things along.

I won't go into every mistake, miscue and gaff that made what should have been a 6-9 month build last over two years and run about 10% over budget. It was December 2021 before we finally closed on the build and it was rent ready. Needless to say, for my military trained mind this endeavor was very nerve wracking. What was the root cause for the ridiculously long build? A global pandemic, poor project management and quality control as well as a unique socio-economic environment where demand for workers far outweighs supply are all likely suspects.

Regardless, the finished product is as planned and we rented it less than 30 days after closing. Rents have skyrocketed during the build and the new units demand a premium. Are we losing return on our out of pocket investment on this build in the near term? Absolutely. However, in the long run, the math works out and we should come out pretty well on this investment.

To put it in program management terms, performance was met but cost and schedule were completely blown. Which brings me to the crux of this section, when building you get what you pay for. We went with the lowest bidder and the schedule suffered for it. An old saying in the acquisition world goes you can have it quick, good and cheap…pick two.

Would we build again? It depends. Timing is everything and even though the build took for what seemed like forever, the timing was quite by accident, superb. Most of the materials were procured at pre-inflation prices so the overall cost of the build was substantially less than what it would cost to build today. The property appraised much higher than what we built it for, giving instant equity. We were able to also lock in a great interest rate on the permanent loan and even get some cash out. Not sure we could do the same in 2022.

Rents also increased dramatically over the two years during the build due to a lot of reasons making the property more profitable. If the property was completed on time, the rent would be lower. Lastly, existing real estate prices have gone through the roof in our area recently. We could not purchase a comparable property already built for what we paid for this construction.

All that being said, I think we are definitely more lucky than good. I'm not sure I want to press my luck again. I'm a bit anxious by nature and this build was a very trying experience. If schedule delays and a host of other problems near daily are something that might cause your anxiety to peg, building might not be the best option! Even though I got several more grey hairs as a result of this build, it was a tremendous learning experience. If we do ever undertake another build, we know the questions to ask and what to look for, whether building another investment property or our dream home. We will definitely be a bit more deliberate in choosing a builder and more directly involved in project management of the build.

Setting Rent and Security Deposits

Before going out and finding that first tenant, the investor must make an important decision, how much to charge in rent! When determining rent there are several items to consider including "class" of the property, location, amenities and age of the home to name a few. I've already shared that one of our business practices is to rent slightly below market. I also shared in the preceding section that a new construction rental home will demand a premium. Like most things in this business, setting rent is common sense. But what exactly does "market rent" mean?

As part of selecting the best property, the investor should have completed analysis and understand the market rate for the class of property under consideration. In other words, setting rent should be completed long before running the first ad! An investor better have a good idea what they will charge in rent when signing the purchase contract! But let's pull on this thread a little more and talk "class" of property.

I never really liked using the word class in association with rental homes as it contains perhaps some negative connotations. Regardless, it is worth a review. There are many definitions for rental property classes, but generally speaking, Class "A" properties are those large, modern complexes located in the hottest part of town that are professionally managed and pull the highest rents in the area. Class "B" properties may be small complexes, duplexes, quadraplexes or single family homes that are actively managed but may be located a little further out of town and may not feature the same level of amenities at that of a Class "A" property. Finally, Class "C" simply put is low rent housing. Class C properties are usually always located in less desirable parts of town and feature only the bare necessities for tenants.

We've found Class B is the sweet spot for the amateur investor. Class C properties will probably introduce more challenges than the weekend warrior investor will want to deal with and most of us aren't resourced well enough to dive into Class A properties. There is a large market of renters for class B properties as many folks can't or won't pay the high rents in a Class A property and don't want to live in bare bones, low rent housing.

So how does this translate to setting rent? It is important to know market rent for the three classes and set rent accordingly for the property you own. This information can easily be found on apartment finder websites. Set the rent too high and you may price yourself out of the market. Too low and you may attract the wrong renters. Nowadays is a bit of an anomaly. In many markets, demand for rentals far outweighs supply so it's a landlords market. Some investors are getting greedy and gouging rents higher than their class of rental property should support. This is why it is important to establish those principles that will guide your operation as we previously discussed!

Using today's current red hot rental market as an example, we have a few units with long term tenants that are currently paying rent well below market for the type of property. While we are slowly increasing rent, we are resisting the urge to gouge up to current market rates. Our tenants respect this and also know they can't find a new home near what they are paying now. Long term tenants are a good thing in the business. Setting rent at a fair but appropriate rate at the outset is crucial to finding and keeping long term tenants.

I've talked about external factors in setting rent, probably more importantly are the internal factors. How much is the mortgage, insurance and property taxes? What are expected maintenance or repair costs and is there an HOA fee on the property? These are all examples of expenses that must be considered when setting rent. Again, the investor should have performed most of this calculus at the outset when determining capitalization rate and shopping for the property so it should be just a matter of tweaking a few numbers before putting a figure in that first advertisement. It should go without saying, but the object of rental property investing is to make money. Set the rent to cover all expenses and if possible, make some monthly income!

Lastly, a word on security deposits. This may seem like an insignificant topic but one we definitely screwed up when we started! Our initial though process was that a low security deposit (half of monthly rent) would entice more prospective tenants because of the low upfront out of pocket costs. While our logic proved true, there was also a terrible downside! Too low of a security deposit offers no motivation for the tenant to leave the property in acceptable condition upon move out. It is fairly easy for most tenants to walk away from a $500 security deposit if it means they don't have to clean or repair anything. Tenants are more focused when security deposits are set at $1000 or more.

We found ourselves losing a lot of money when tenants moved out as they would leave the residence in rough shape and simply walk out on their low security deposit. The low security deposit didn't come close to covering the cost to reset the property. We learned our lesson. Now we collect a security deposit equal to one month's rent and have already noticed a difference. Tenants will at least make an attempt to leave the property in good condition in order to retrieve some of their deposit back. Some landlords will ask for even more than one month's rent in security deposit. Be sure to check local laws as there are sometimes caps set on security deposits.

Perhaps yet again the realistic tone in my delivery could discourage real estate investing! Trust me, it is not as hard as it sounds. My wife and I are naturally risk adverse. If the odds weren't overwhelmingly stacked in our favor for success, we wouldn't have purchased any of the properties we own. Location is key. If a property is just not located in an area where people want to live, it will be slow to rent and bring low rents until something changes. I think sometimes people wear blinders to this stark reality. That cute 1920's cottage might be the perfect rental. But if its location is in an undesirable area and it costs twice what you are paying for it to rehab, then it really doesn't matter how cute the home is. Unlike buying a personal residence, investment real estate purchases are business decisions, not emotional ones.

Or more simply put, to use my favorite analogy, buying real estate is a math problem. The math is called determining capitalization rate. I provided an example of one way to figure cap rate, there are several others. Choose the one that works best for you and do the math! The numbers don't lie.

Many people probably stay away from rental properties due to the perceived cost of repairs. This risk is mitigated when selecting the best property. The big stuff is obvious, a home inspector will help you find the little stuff. That being said, "Murphy's Law," which in simple terms states what can go wrong will go wrong, is alive and well. A property that checks out clean may blow an HVAC the first month of ownership. On the flip side, you may own the property 10 years before spending one dime on a major repair. My wife and I have experienced both of these scenarios in our 14 years in the business.

Before leaving this section I'd like to clarify and expand on one topic that I touched on previously but kind of blew past. In the section on cap rate I provided an example where I suggested that $400000 was too high asking price for a duplex in an area that would only produce a maximum of $1200 per unit in rent. Let's say it is the only multi-family that's been on the market in the area in over a year. Should we make an offer anyway? No! The math just doesn't work and this is a business decision.

However, add the property to your watch list. Perhaps if the property sits on the market for 90 or 120 days the seller may get eager to sell. After doing some capitalization rate math, you might find $320000 would provide an acceptable return and who knows the seller might accept a lower offer! Remember, when real estate investing, the investor must work to get to yes!

The condition of a structure, bank loans and even location are all fixed variables or to use the expression "known, knowns". These factors can and must be planned for to successfully run a rental property business. But what about the other major factor in the rental property business? The one that is about as unpredictable as the day is long. Of course I am talking about the human factor. Read on to learn how we establish a relationship with tenants!

Chapter 4: Establishing a Relationship with Tenants

My assumption is many folks steer clear of real estate investing because it is inherently a people business. Whether working with a real estate agent while searching for the best property, talking to the loan officer at the bank or responding to a tenant's request for repairs, owning rental property requires near constant interaction with fellow humans. Working with a bank or real estate agent is the easy part! As you probably guessed, the challenging people side of the rental property business is developing a relationship with tenants.

Although I served as a leader in the military for nearly a quarter century, on a Meyers Briggs personality type indicator, I usually show as a high performing introvert. It doesn't come natural for me to engage, persuade and sometimes confront other people. Unfortunately, my wife is exactly the same.

That being said, we've learned over the years how to communicate effectively with tenants, from the moment they arrive as a prospect, to the time they move out. There is really no secret to good tenant – landlord relations. Landlord – tenant relationships are an ongoing process that starts from the moment a landlord offers a property for rent, to when a tenant moves out, sometimes a number of years later.

Advertising and Showing

Today, there are many great websites and social media marketplaces to advertise. Long gone are the days of running an ad in the paper. Most of these services are fairly low cost or often free. We started initially listing on Craigslist, then social media marketplaces and now we use one of the major rental listing services which charges $10 a week to advertise on their site. I can't remember the last time we had a property listed over a week!

Like most things, you get what you pay for. Using a paid service to list on the apartment finder sites will weed out a lot of the trolls and prank calls you get when listing for free on Craigslist or social media. Picking which advertising outlet is really up to personal preference and what you are comfortable with. In just about every market, as soon as the listing is posted, be prepared, as the phone will start blowing up!

More critical than which advertising outlet to choose, is posting great pictures of the property in the ad. Thankfully, my wife is skilled at taking pictures and she has a better camera on her smart phone. A picture is worth a thousand words and we usually post at least 10-12 pics of both the interior and exterior of the home. The first picture on the ad should always be the best as that is the one displayed on the listing. Some sites offer many other options such as 360 views and virtual tours, just depends on how creative you want to be!

Although the pics are worth a thousand words, when listing a property, there still has to be an accompanying narrative that describes the property accurately and entices prospective tenants to make the call. I usually handle the advert writing since, as you may have noticed, I rather enjoy writing! Below is the text from one of our advertisements. All of our ads follow the same basic concept- hook, glowing description of features and encouraging the call.

Example Ad Narrative:
Over 1200 newly remodeled square feet in this wonderfully located 3BR/2BA duplex home! Quiet living but just 15

minutes from jobs and amenities thanks to quick access at the convergence of three major roads. Zoned for (name) Elementary and (name) Middle / High schools! Brand new carpet, paint, 2" blinds, and all stainless steel appliances to include over the counter microwave as well as fridge with ice / water! This two story home also includes laminate wood flooring, washer & dryer, ceiling fans and a big back yard. At $XXX per month this one won't last long, call to see this great home today!

Once the ad is up, be prepared to start fielding inquiries immediately! Some of these will be "trolls" for lack of a better term, who are not really interested in the property. Most prospective tenants will initiate contact via text or email which is perfectly fine. However, we have a standing rule that we will not set up an appointment to show the property until the prospect calls. This is also a great way to make the initial introductions and break the ice.

Before showing any property, we ensure it is spotless and in perfect working order. First impressions are important but what we've discovered is that prospective tenants who would be ok with moving into a less than ready home, may not be the best tenants. Like most things in the rental business, there is always a measure of risk when showing properties. Occasionally a prospect won't show up, won't call or respond to calls. Maybe they went in a different direction or perhaps they were trolling.

Regardless, the first actual showing is always exciting and a little scary! My wife shows our properties and we stick to set security procedures. She sends me her calendar with appointments that include who she is meeting and when. She checks in with me before and after the appointment. As stated, she always voice verifies prospects prior to making an appointment; never make an appointment via text! During the appointment, she follows basic security rules such as remaining between the prospective tenant and the exit door, never turning her back, as well as other common sense measures.

Thankfully, she has never had any bad encounters after literally hundreds of showings. We maintain a positive world view and believe strongly people are inherently good. Most folks are just looking for a new place to call home. Often times, prospective tenants are apprehensive about meeting us! There are a lot of scams these days that target folks looking to rent. We've all seen the news. Unfortunately, there are just a very few dangerous people out there. Caution is a must when showing rental properties.

My wife's routine is to let the property show itself, yet another advantage of having the home spotless and in perfect working order before listing. She will answer questions and engage in small talk to get a feel for the prospective tenant but again, really no "selling". We've found our homes will be a good fit for a prospective tenant or it won't. They will let you know! For those who do wish to apply, we fill out the rental application on site. Which brings us to our next section and probably the most important task to establishing a relationship with tenants...

Screening

Once a prospective tenant is interested in a property, we use both a standard rental application as well as an online tenant screening service offered by one of the major credit reporting companies. Our application is a pretty standard format that includes the applicant's signature for authorization to seek employment and residence information. If the prospective tenant is accepted, then the application becomes part of that tenants file. Very important to point out that the application is full of the applicant's Personally Identifiable Information and must be safeguarded. For those prospective tenants that are not selected but qualified, we will hang on to the application for about 30 days (in case anything falls through with the selected applicant) and then destroy the application.

The data on the application complements the online screening I'll review in just a moment. We always verify employment and current residence per the information provided on the application. Many employers require an on line employment verification process that can get a little complicated but it is worth the effort! Similarly, most landlords will require a copy of the applicant's release of information before they will share information about the individual.

In either case, we aren't looking for a life history. In the case of employment, we simply verify the applicant is employed where they say they are on the application. For the landlord reference, we usually ask one simple question, "would you rent to them again"? The answer will tell you pretty much everything you need to know! Important to note, as property managers, we often receive requests from other landlords where one of our current or former tenants may be applying for residence. For our great tenants, it is always a pleasure to give a positive review!

Like most things in this book, there are 100's of different rental application formats one can use. There are even completely digital applications offered by some of the bigger apartment finder websites. We are just not that tech savvy yet. Pick the one that meets your needs! The following is a standard application form we use. I retrieved this off an internet site some years ago. More importantly, take note of the information we collect. This is probably a good baseline for tenant screening.

RENTAL APPLICATION

APPLICANT INFORMATION

Name:		DOB:
SSN#:	Email:	Mobile PH:
Driver's License #:	State Issued:	Work PH:

CURRENT ADDRESS: City: State: Zip:

☐ Own (or) ☐ Rent? | Monthly Rent: | Landlord Name & Phone:
From ____ to Present | Reason for Leaving:
Were you ever late to pay rent? ☐ YES ☐ NO | If YES, explain:

PREVIOUS ADDRESS: City: State: Zip:

☐ Own (or) ☐ Rent? | Monthly Rent: | Landlord Name & Phone:
From ____ to ____ | Reason for Leaving:
Were you ever late to pay rent? ☐ YES ☐ NO | If YES, explain:

EMPLOYMENT INFORMATION

Current Employer:	Phone:
Address:	Position:
☐ Hourly (or) ☐ Salary?	Hourly Rate:	Monthly income:	How long employed w/employer?
Manager/Supervisor Name:	Mgr. Phone:	Mgr. Email:

FINANCIAL INFORMATION

| Name of Bank | PH: | Type of Account(s) |
| Current Monthly Financial Obligations: ☐ Car $____ ☐ Credit $____ ☐ Loan $____ ☐ Other $____ |
| Have you ever filed for bankruptcy? ☐ YES ☐ NO | How do you prefer to pay rent: ☐ Check ☐ Online / Zelle |

PERSONAL BACKGROUND & HISTORY

In the past seven (7) years, have you been convicted of, or do you currently have any charges pending for, any criminal offense? ☐ YES ☐ NO If Yes, Explain ____

Have you ever been evicted or do you currently owe any money to a landlord for any reason? ☐ YES ☐ NO If Yes, Explain ____

Are you a smoker? ☐ YES ☐ NO | Do you have Renter's Insurance? ☐ YES ☐ NO | Do you keep ANY pets? ☐ YES ☐ NO If Yes, Describe: ____

OCCUPANCY INFORMATION

Besides applicant, list any other adults/children who plan to stay at the residence. Anyone listed 18 or over who is not a dependent of the applicant must complete a separate rental application and sign all documents (use back of application for additional space):

Name: ____ Relationship: ____ Age: ____
Name: ____ Relationship: ____ Age: ____

CONSENT to RELEASE INFORMATION

I CERTIFY to the best of my knowledge that all statements in this application are true. Any false, fraudulent, or misleading information provided on this application may be grounds for denial of tenancy and/or termination of your lease agreement.
I hereby AUTHORIZE the Landlord, both for initial tenancy and again upon any future lease modifications or renewals, to obtain and verify all information provided on this application by obtaining credit reports, collecting civil/criminal records and character reports, verifying employment status and income, and confirming rental history.

Print ____ Sign ____ Date ____

In addition to the standard application, we use an online screening service provided by one of the major credit reporting agencies. The current cost for this service is $40 and we collect the application fee from the prospective tenant (in cash only) when they fill out the application. All adult, non-family members who intend to reside in the residence must also apply and pay the $40 for screening (more on this situation in just a moment). It is quite an easy process! Once a landlord sets up a property in the account, it is simply a matter of inputting the prospective tenant's email address to initiate the online application. The service does the rest and provides a detailed report based on the information provided by the applicant. In addition to credit history which contains such details as open credit lines, collections and bankruptcy history, the tenant screening service also provides criminal and eviction history.

The service provides a numerical residents score (not exactly the same as a credit score) and a recommendation to either accept or decline the applicant. We usually try to find at least 4 or 5 applicants when listing a property as there may be applicants who come back "decline" or some will change their mind after applying. Often there may be more than one applicant who receives an "accept" recommendation from the tenant screening service. In this case we go to the provided numerical score and select the applicant with the highest number. On very rare occasions, two applicants may have the same score and recommendation. It this instance, the decision may come down to who submitted their application first. First and best applicant per the tenant screening is our business practice.

It's always tough but we contact each applicant and let them know their status. Most will take a decline good naturedly but some may become upset. The screening service has the option to download the report and in some cases we've provided the applicant with the report we receive so they can understand what may be holding them back. We have to choose the best qualified applicant based on their screening score. Once a candidate is selected via the screening service, as previously mentioned, we use the employment and residence references on the traditional application as a final verification.

A quick note on Equal Housing Opportunity. By law, rental property investors managing their own properties must make fair decisions when selecting tenants. Discrimination based on race, sex, religion, sexual orientation is not just

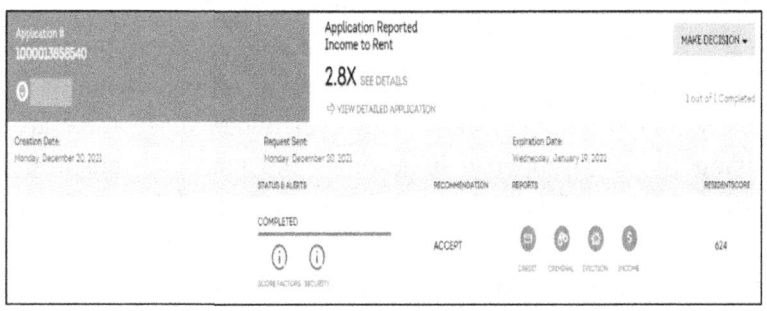

wrong, it is illegal. That is why we love using a tenant screening service as it makes the selection process quantifiable based on the data provided by the service. Above is a screen shot of the summary report.

  The selection process takes time but is probably the most critical step of owning and renting properties. Fortunately, we've gotten it correct more than we've gotten it wrong! Despite the best efforts to screen tenants, there will be the occasional tenant who just won't live up to their end of the contract. More on managing bad tenants coming up!

Signing the Lease

Some tenants may not fully understand that a lease is a written contract between themselves and the landlord with legal implications and responsibilities (that goes both ways). That is why the leasing step of property management is so critical. There are several places to acquire a lease format, probably a quick online search would reveal many. Additionally, this may be a good time to use an online legal service site that will crank out a custom lease tailored for a small fee. Above all, the lease must contain the legal requirements for the particular state in which the property is located. For this reason, I am not going to paste a screen shot of the lease we use or cover the multiple paragraphs of legalese that a lease must contain. What I will review are the portions of a lease that we have learned, mostly the hard way, are important.

First and foremost, determine who needs to sign the lease. Today, there are a myriad of living arrangements. It is really none of our business! However, when those folks are living in your property, it becomes the landlords business. Any adult non-family member who resides on the premises (i.e. roommate, girlfriend, boyfriend, common in law spouse, whatever) should sign the lease. Furthermore, we also require these adult occupants to apply as a co-applicant during the screening process. Co-applicants require another $40 fee for the screening service we use.

It is important to be very upfront with prospective and selected tenants on this topic when discussing the lease. This applies to adult occupants who may move into the premises after the initial signing but during the term of the lease. Of course, immediate family members of the tenant do not have to sign the lease, but their names and relationships should be recorded in the appropriate portion of the lease document.

Why is this such a big deal? Once an adult establishes residence in a home, they have certain legal rights. Let's say a tenant decides to have their girlfriend / boyfriend move in with them and the landlord just turns a blind eye by not placing the new non familial occupant on the lease. If some months later the tenant abandons the premises but their (former) significant other remains, then the landlord has a real situation on their hands. The landlord has no legal contract with the person occupying the property, but the individual possesses some rights to occupancy as the home is established as their residence. They may or may not feel compelled to pay rent! Additionally, the eviction process just got a whole lot messier.

The second most important portion of the lease is the rent, namely, when it is due, how much and what are the late penalties. Most leases will contain language such as "due on the first, late after the fifth" or words to that effect. If so, just know, 99.9% of tenants will not pay rent until the fifth. Ensure tenants understand the paragraph regarding late fees and when the eviction process will be initiated due to non-payment. This should all be spelled out in the lease, with all the required legalese. Additionally, when my wife signs a lease with a tenant she will review these sections carefully. More on collecting rent coming up!

The third most important item to cover is the paragraph regarding pets. There should be no question whether or not pets are allowed on the premises and the penalties for bringing them without the owner's permission. Technically, introducing pets into the home when none are allowed is a breach of contract and the tenant could be evicted. More than likely the tenants and landlord can work out an agreement but realize this is a topic the average rental investor *will* have to address at some point in their rental property investing career.

Lastly is a paragraph regarding improvements. If the property has a yard, many tenants may want to put in a storage shed or kid's outdoor activities (above ground pool, swing set, trampoline). If this is the case, a tenant must request these improvements in *writing*. We require the tenant to sign an addendum that states they are responsible for placing, upkeep and removing the improvement. The addendum also includes a "hold harmless" clause. We also require these tenants to maintain a renter's insurance policy and provide us a copy when the premium renews.

Same applies for indoor improvements such as mounting a TV to a wall or adding a cable drop to a room. The bottom line is when a tenant signs the lease they must understand they are required to *ask in writing* before performing any improvement on the property. You may ask, why even allow a tenant to place an improvement on the property? The answer is simple, a tenant who makes the home their own is likely to stay there long term. I'll talk more about the human factor coming up.

A quick word on tenant provided renters insurance. Currently, our lease does not require tenants to maintain rental insurance unless we've authorized them to place improvements on the property. In the lease, we do highly suggest that tenants gain renters insurance under all circumstances. Requiring tenants to maintain liability insurance is yet another level of protecting your asset we'll talk about in more detail later in the book.

Other items we spell out very clearly in our lease includes tenant required maintenance such as HVAC filters, bulbs and lawn care. Tenant required repairs, namely clogged toilets / drains, is important to cover. You would be surprised how many tenants think they can stop up a commode and then have the landlord pay to fix it for them! Tenants must understand drains they clogged, or any damage to the property, through their own negligence are their responsibility to fix.

Parking is a big one, especially for condo type properties. On the subject of condos, it is important to attach a copy of the condo house or HOA rules and make adhering to the rules a condition of the lease. We've had a few challenges with this over the years. Lastly, it is always good to cover expectations about hanging things on the wall and window treatments.

Generally there will be an "Additional Provisions" section of the lease which is the catch all where the landlord can spell out or amplify on any particular requirements for the tenant. The following is an example of an additional provisions section from a lease for one of our condo units.

Example Additional Provisions:
ADDITIONAL PROVISIONS; DISCLOSURES.
Paragraph 7: every effort must be made to hang pictures without penetrating walls
Paragraph 10: utilities included are water, sewer and trash removal
Paragraph 11g: Tenant is responsible for changing HVAC filter monthly and light bulbs as needed
Paragraph 11l: Tenant and guests must abide by the enclosed condominium house and parking rules. Failure to comply could result in fines or termination of lease agreement.
Paragraph 19: Landlord highly recommends tenant gains a renter's insurance policy
Upon move out, condo must be returned in condition received or tenant will be charged for cleaning fees and repairs.

How does the average landlord know to cover all these things in a lease? Well hopefully this book will help! But most real estate investors like us had to learn the hard way, through trial and error. Experience is often the best teacher. Our lease agreements are continually evolving, I don't think any two look the same! To ensure the tenants read each page, we ask them to initial at the bottom of each page in addition to their signature on the last page of the document. Of course, we initial the bottom of each page as well, which is our word that we will live up to our portion of the lease, critical to....

Keeping Tenants Content

So now we've got a new tenant, what's next? First and foremost, treat everyone with dignity and respect. My wife and I pride ourselves on offering clean, well maintained and

MOVE-IN / MOVE OUT INSPECTION CHECKLIST

Tenant Name: _____
Apartment Address: _____
Date: _____

Area / Item	Condition @ move-in	Condition @ exit	Est. Repair Cost
KITCHEN			
Floors / floor covering			
Walls & ceiling			
Windows / locks / Window coverings			
Doors / knobs			
Light fixtures / bulbs			
Cabinets/cupboards/she			
Drawers / countertops			
Sinks / stoppers / Drains / plumbing			
APPLIANCES			
Stove / Oven			
Outside			
Burners			
Drip pans			
Hood vent			
Timer / controls			
Broiler pan			
Lights			
Refrigerator			
Outside			
Inside			
Dishwasher			
Garbage disposal			
Trash compactor			
Laundry equipment			
Other appliances			
LIVING ROOM			
Floors / floor covering			
Walls & ceiling			
Windows / locks / Window coverings			
Doors / locks			
Light fixtures / bulbs			
Closet / shelves			
Fireplace			
DINING ROOM			
Floors / floor covering			
Walls & ceiling			
Windows / locks / Window coverings			
Doors / locks			
Light fixtures / bulbs			
Closet / shelves			

affordable rental homes. She does the showing, lease paperwork and day to day management while I work maintenance and repair issues. We both interact with our tenants with courtesy and professionalism. "Yes ma'am / No sir" are the norms. And guess what? Our tenants mirror that behavior right back at us!

Upon move in, we conduct and sign a joint walk through inspection of the property. Most likely, the tenant didn't notice a lightly stained carpet when initially shown the property. A detailed joint inspection serves as a mutual agreement to the condition of the property and is an important starting point for setting expectations for both the landlord and tenant. See the sample of the inspection checklist we use above.

So the tenants are in, now what? The easiest way to summarize this aspect of rental property management is, life happens. There may be months of smooth sailing and then an air conditioner will break, typically on the hottest day of the year. Pipes will begin leaking on Saturday night. Key to keeping tenants content is to respond quickly to every maintenance request. For the easy stuff, I will take care of the problem as soon as I leave my day job or on the weekend. For the bigger issues, we have a list of service providers that usually respond quickly. Tenants are essentially paying landlords for a service they do not wish to handle themselves, maintain the residence. I'll talk more about maintaining the property next chapter!

There are also those other aspects of tenant - landlord life that just happen. Jobs are lost, people move on, a global pandemic occurs and as has happened to us (twice now) sometimes a tenant may pass away. Compassion will rule the day. If a tenant lost their job and is going to be a little late on rent, better to work out something with them than go the eviction route. When a tenant gets sick or as we had happen, expires, communication is critical. Always maintain emergency contact information for tenants!

I'll share the story of one of our tenants who passed as an example. She was a very sweet, older lady who lived alone. I knew she was not in the best of health but also knew she had a good social network through her church that kept tabs on her. One Sunday night, just a few days before Christmas, we got a call from one of her church friends who was concerned because she had not been able to contact our tenant.

I was very thankful for the call. When someone calls emergency services for a health and welfare, the fire department will bust down the door which generally entails replacing the door frame (yes, we've had that happen before). I met our tenant's friend at the residence with the key and we banged loudly on the door with no response. We used the key to enter and unfortunately found our tenant in the floor alive but unresponsive. We called 911 but she passed in the hospital the next day.

When our tenant's daughter came from out of state to settle her mom's estate, we let her stay in the residence free for a month. You see, I am no psychologist but I believe our tenant was a hoarder. The rooms were stacked floor to ceiling with goods she had purchased via online shopping. I knew it would take her daughter and friend a few weeks to get everything sorted out. They did a great job removing the contents and cleaning up. Our simple act of kindness during this tragedy was returned to us almost immediately.

If an investor's margins are so slim that they can't swing a month or two of free rent or worse yet, they feel compelled to shake down a tenant who is struggling with a legitimate challenge, then perhaps rental property investing isn't a good fit. We have worked with private charitable organizations and local government agencies to help our tenants get enrolled in rental assistance programs. Sometimes this means receiving the rent three or four weeks late. But at the end of the day, this is a people business.

In addition to treating our tenants with dignity and respect, we try to make little gestures such as holiday cards with small gift certificates. Sometimes I'll help a tenant unclog that toilet (even though it's their responsibility) and generally conduct ourselves as the service providers we are.

Why go out of our way? Well beyond dignity and respect being a value we espouse, there is a payoff. Content tenants will stay longer which reduces the money spent on repairs thusly increasing profits over time. Turning over tenants every year will cut heavily into a rental unit's return on investment. Keeping a content tenant for three years or longer is solid gold!

The overwhelming majority of tenants we've had over the past 14 years were exceptional folks. They reciprocated our professionalism and we remain in contact with some even after they move out. But, like every people business, there is unfortunately that very small but visible segment of tenants that makes the rental property business occasionally very frustrating. More on the bad apples coming up!

Collecting Rent

It might not seem intuitive that a task as routine as collecting rent money would warrant its own section but it absolutely does! I am not talking about collecting rent in the general sense, but rather the actual physical means for getting rent money from the tenant's pocket to the investors account. Believe it or not, this can get screwed up and when it does, it is an absolute mess. Over the past 14 years we've tried a variety of ways to collect rent money with varying degrees of success. I'll share our lessons learned!

I'll review in upcoming chapters how property management companies make bookkeeping and growing a real estate investment more manageable. Collecting rent is also an area where using a trustworthy property management company can simplify a sometimes challenging task. For our properties managed by a property management company, they do all the leg work of collecting rent money. They generally have well established processes, mostly of the autopay variety.

The funds just show up automatically every month in our account accompanied by an email with a detailed, itemized statement by unit! Of course, the management company takes their cut for providing this service. Expect to pay 10%-15% monthly when using a property management company.

If the investor is actively managing a property, then collecting rent money each month is something that must be managed carefully. We started collecting rent years ago entirely by paper means but have now transitioned nearly entirely too automated payments. There are a few pros and cons for both.

When collecting paper checks you'll either have to meet the tenant every month or rely on the mail service. We've done both. Paper checks provide the most accurate record and security for the transfer of funds for both the tenant and landlord. If a check is lost in the mail, the tenant can stop payment and reissue. The cancelled check on both the tenant and landlords bank statement provides probably the best record for the exchange of funds. Of course, rent checks can and do bounce from time to time! There are fees associated both with the tenants and landlords bank account when a check bounces. It is important to know your bank's policy on bounced checks and have a plan for addressing when it *does* happen.

Next I'll talk money orders. We were surprised to learn that some tenants do not maintain checking accounts! Probably not a legitimate reason to not offer a tenant a lease if qualified, but certainly something to be aware of. We've had a few over the years that preferred to pay rent by money orders. The pro of this method is that money orders are essentially the same as cash without all the risk of holding a wad of bills. The downside is, like cash, if lost, stolen or otherwise mishandled, it is harder for the tenant or landlord to recoup funds from a money order. On that note, a quick word on cash.

We do not accept cash payments for rent. There is just too much risk involved on a lot of different levels. For the protection of both our interests and the tenants, we stick with paper or electronic payment of rent.

Our preferred method of rent payment is via electronic means and as an indicator of the times, of our current 17 tenants all but one use electronic means to pay rent. Electronic payment is quick, easy and does not require a lot of extra work on either parties' part. Electronic payment is not without risk. Important to point out, not all electronic payment methods are created equal. We prefer to use the money transfer service associated with our bank. As long as the tenant's bank also uses this service, then transfers are quick and easy as well as more traceable for the protection of both parties.

The numerous "cash" applications available are another means of electronic payment. We use these from time to time but "cash" apps are less preferred because the increased risk of an error in payment. As with any non-physical means of payment, the biggest risk of electronic rent payment is a glitch in the transfer. Using a cash app could increase this risk if the tenant were to contend, "well I sent the payment yesterday" yet the landlord never received the funds. In most cases, this would be a nightmare to hunt down! Thankfully, we have not encountered this challenge…yet.

There are other electronic means to transfer funds, including wires, establishing deposit only access for tenants to the landlord's bank accounts and a few others. There are pros and cons to each. Unlike physical rent payment where we provide a standard receipt to the tenant, payment by electronic means is usually only confirmed by a quick "thanks I got the rent" text from the landlord to the tenant.

Finally, a quick word on credit cards. We are set up to accept credit cards but in 14 years, have never accepted a rent payment via credit card. Credit cards for rent is just a bad idea all the way around, especially for tenants. The only reason we set up the ability to accept credit cards is as a last ditch option to pay rent before we would begin the eviction process. Thankfully, we've never had to cross that bridge.

There are a lot of nuances to the actual collection of rent. As previously mentioned, if in the lease, rent is due on the first and late on the fifth, then 99.9% of the time the landlord can expect the tenant to either date a check for the 5th or initiate the electronic transfer on the 5th. It's just human nature; certainly what I used to do when I paid rent! This may mean the actual funds won't hit the landlords account until a few days later. This is something an investor will need to plan for as they map out their own payment of monthly mortgage, insurance or other expenses. While habitually paying on the 5th could be addressed with the tenant, I always advise to pick your battles. If the rent is coming in, probably not worth raising an issue about it arriving on the 5th or even a day or two after if stuck in bank processing.

Another tactic we've seen some tenants use is to provide several months or even a year's worth of pre filled checks. This is a pretty clever way for a tenant to lock in their rent rate beyond their lease agreement, especially if they are month to month. Of course the fix to this is to just not accept pre-filled checks that extend beyond the expiration of the current lease. We have fell for this one a time or two!

A quick word on month to month. Generally, after the time frame on a lease is up there is a "holdover" clause whereby the tenant can continue to pay rent month to month. Usually the tenancy can be broken with 30 days written notice by either party. Check your local laws! There are a few advantages to this arrangement. Tenants love it as it gives them flexibility to move any time with 30 days' notice.

Similarly, it gives the landlord some options if they wish to terminate the tenancy.

But there are a few drawbacks. Namely, if you want to go up on the rent you'll need to sign a new lease. If the tenant has been paying month to month for a long while, they will probably not be thrilled to sign a new lease. We've done it both ways, gone month to month and required tenants to sign a new lease upon their initial lease expiration. As long as the landlord is alert, prepared and communicating well with the tenant, either method works.

Lastly, a word on government subsidized rents. Currently our properties are not enrolled in Section 8 housing programs. Perhaps it is a sign of the times, but the first question many prospective tenants will ask is if the property is eligible for Section 8. Many investors readily seek Section 8 opportunities but it is just not something we have explored. There are a few government hoops an investor must go through to enroll a property as Section 8. In theory, it is a great concept. Renters use government funded section 8 vouchers to pay for a portion or all of their rent. Many investors love participating in this program.

We have on several occasions had tenants participate in public and private rent relief funds. The tenant will show a need to an organization whether public or private and the organization will pay the tenants rent. This takes some coordination and will usually mean the rent won't arrive on the first, but we readily participate in these programs. Understanding and working with tenants when they've experienced some serious challenges is another one of our core values / business practices.

The big takeaway on this section is to have a plan to collect rent, not just in the general sense but in the literal sense. Consider all the nuances of this seemingly simple task. Think about your rent plan before your month to month tenant hands you a fist full of pre-filled checks! Electronic is easiest but not all electronic payment means are the same and must be monitored carefully to ensure no problems. Avoid cash and money orders when possible as there is little recourse if the payment is lost or stolen. Collecting rent is not quite as easy as one would think!

Managing Bad Tenants

There is an old saying in the Army that goes, "you spend 95% of your time on 5% of your Soldiers". The implication, it takes leaders a lot of time dealing with the 5% of bad Soldiers, usually to the detriment of your 95% good Soldiers. I believe this same adage holds true for tenants. Despite the best screening efforts, as I've previously mentioned, life happens and there are rotten apples in every bunch. Again, dignity and respect but with the addition of firmness will take the day. First and foremost, ensure a good understanding of the laws in the state which the property is located. Most are pretty straight forward and spell out tenant as well as landlord rights during the eviction process.

Tenants don't want to get evicted and while we have encountered some habitual slow payers, who seem willing to pay our $50 late fee frequently, we've only experienced a couple of renters who got in a situation where they absolutely could not pay rent. In these cases, we explain in very clear terms the eviction process and help them understand that an eviction is a court ordered judgement that will follow them around for years hindering their ability to secure quality housing in the future.

In each case, they have chosen to just abandon the premises rather than face the eviction process. While we lost a little money on these cases, the unit is cleared and we can turn the property for a new renter relatively quickly. In my opinion, having a tenant abandon a property with a small short term loss is a better option than going through the sometimes lengthy court process to evict.

What about tenants who just aren't living up to the terms of the lease agreement? This could include subletting the property, not performing tenant required maintenance or just keeping the property in an unclean or unsafe condition. Again, check local laws first but we've found most people respond well to firm but fair communications. Show them the paragraph in their signed, legally binding contract where they agreed not to exhibit the bad behaviors. Remind them that a breach of this contract could be grounds for an eviction process and all the negative aspects that come with it. We've found most folks will comply.

I shared earlier about our tenant who was most likely a hoarder. Certainly not something you can tell from a screening process! As you may recall, she was a sweet, elderly lady. Thankfully, most of her hoarding was items she bought off home shopping...and never unpacked! Boxes were neatly stacked floor to ceiling in two of the three bedrooms in her apartment. What could we do? Kick her out? Whenever I went into the residence for a maintenance issue, I inspected to ensure there were no fire or other safety concerns. I personally helped her tidy up a few times. Certainly this was a case of "it is what it is" in the landlord business.

After 24 years in the military and 14 years of rental property business, I don't get surprised much anymore. On occasion though, there are scenarios that pop up truly beyond belief. I will provide one such example that occurred just last year.

One fine summer morning I was conducting some maintenance at one of our duplexes when I noticed our tenant approaching the driveway in a moving truck. I asked him what's up and he replied he was moving...today. Still under a valid lease, I of course immediately inquired, "when were you going to tell us" and "why are you moving"? He didn't have a good answer to the first question, I fully expect he was just going to skip out. But it was the answer to the "why" that got me. He replied, "Those people are driving me crazy."

Turns out, "those people" were a mother / grown son con artist couple who had gained entrance into the house under the premise of providing care for our tenant who had some medical issues. In reality, they were ex-cons and addicts with a rap sheet a mile long. Not only did he fall for their con, he was about to ditch the property and leave these two people in our house!

The tenant removed his things and abandoned the premises. Note what I said earlier about adults having certain rights when they establish residence. I called the Sheriff's department to see what could be done. The Sheriff's office was empathetic but upfront with the fact that they may not be able to do much. Regardless, they came out to the residence twice to speak with the squatters. Thankfully, most addicts and ex-cons aren't looking to tangle with the law, they took their few possessions and split. It was the best possible outcome for a truly sketchy situation. Once they left, it was one of the few times I exercised my rights as a concealed carry permit holder while working to clean up the rental unit. I was afraid they may come back to start some trouble. Not a good feeling.

The residence which had new paint and carpet when our tenant moved in just a year prior was absolutely trashed. There was unspeakably gross items left all over the residence, doors off the hinges and holes in the wall. Took me two weeks but I finally got the place clean and rent ready again. Thankfully, we got some very nice tenants back into the home.

I am nearly 50 years old and have been blessed with success professionally, personally and financially. As I was cleaning the filth of people who just didn't care, it certainly caused me to take pause and question the motivations for investing in rental properties! The tenant that let the con artists in and abandoned the property passed our screening, his references checked out and he paid rent mostly on time. He was friendly and personable but obviously incredibly naïve. Who could have saw this one coming?

I don't want to end this chapter on establishing a relationship with tenants on a fearful note but I want to share all the good and bad with owning rental properties! As stated in chapter one, diving into rental properties requires a commitment. Not just a financial and time commitment, but the commitment to work in a people business with all that entails. Despite the preceding horror story, I can't stress enough, we've had dozens of great tenants, good people who it was our pleasure to partner with in this profitable business. We still keep in touch with many who have moved on. But the bad apples are out there. As we saw from the story above, some of them probably don't even know they are bad apples, they just get overcome by events!

If you read this chapter and are thinking, "nope, this isn't for me, just too much" I completely understand. I would offer another option that may allow investment in rental properties while avoiding much of the people business. Hire a property management company and let someone else establish a relationship with tenants. Of course the tradeoff is roughly 10%-15% annual loss due to management fees, not to mention the higher maintenance costs when not doing it yourself. In many cases though, the math may still work out in the long run, especially if the property was purchased at the right price!

I will briefly share our positive experience using a property management company in Texas for the past 10+ years.

My wife and I made the plunge into real estate in Killeen, TX in 2008 living in one side of a duplex and renting out the other. No sooner did we arrive to Killeen, I was deployed for a year. One of the upsides to deployments, it offers an opportunity to save a ton of money! This coupled with the income we were making in our first duplex enabled us to save enough to buy another duplex shortly after I returned from deployment.

I got to stay home about seven months before I had to deploy again. While me being out of the picture gave the wife and kids more room in our 1200 square foot duplex home, raising two small children alone and managing two rental properties was taking its toll on her. This is when we established a great relationship with a local property management company that we still maintain today.

There may be times when an investor relocates out of state or due to a change in life circumstances needs to turn over management of a property to a property management company. Expect around a 10% flat fee on gross rental income for management service as well as maintenance coordination fees charged as a percentage of the maintenance bill. Property management companies will handle the eviction process for you if necessary, for a fee of course. Obviously maintenance and repair costs will be much higher when you aren't doing most of it yourself.

Fortunately, there are usually some good property managers in just about every city. For about the 100th time in this book, do the homework! I can't stress enough how positive our experience has been for over a decade with the property management company handling our properties in Texas.

The key is stay in constant communication with the property manager and watch maintenance dollars very carefully. Evaluate constantly. Question everything and understand enough about repairs to know if someone is trying to pull wool over your eyes on costs. Even if everyone is on the up and up, the additional maintenance and management costs may make the math untenable at some point. We've been fortunate to work with a great property manager and are able to keep our distant real estate holdings profitable.

Investing in rental property is inherently unique from other investments in that it is a people business. More specifically, rental investing is about establishing relationships. While tenants are the most important, it is also key to establish relationships with property managers, bankers, plumbers, painters and a host of others. This group collectively helps the investor maintain and eventually grow the investment. Let's dive in to the next chapter on maintaining our real estate investment!

Chapter 5: Maintain the Investment

Much like determining a good location, before purchasing a property, the real estate investor must make an accurate assessment on how much will be required to repair and maintain the property. We talked briefly about how this figures into determining a cap rate for potential investment properties. Before making an offer, the investor should be able to determine the condition of big items at a glance- roof, HVAC, water heater, windows. Also the little stuff that is relatively easy to repair such as paint, blinds, light fixtures, appliances. An investor should know the general cost of repairs, both major and minor. If at least $5k in repairs jumps out immediately when looking at a property, realize there are probably another $5k lurking just under the surface.

In addition to repairs and maintenance, some properties may require monthly Homeowners Association (HOA) dues. These are usually townhouse or condo style properties but may also apply to single family homes in certain subdivisions. An investor should gain a full understanding of what the HOA dues cover and make an assessment if the dues seem reasonable. HOA dues will often cover, water, sewer and trash pickup as well as exterior / common area maintenance and lawn care. We were fortunate to find some condos with fairly priced dues and after deducting expenses from gross rent, we were still able to turn a profit.

Just like an automobile, homes require maintenance and repairs. As we discussed last chapter, this is essentially what a tenant is paying the landlord to do, maintain the property so they don't have to. Fortunately, with rental properties, an investor can leverage their maintenance and repair expenses at tax time to make the investment more profitable. We'll dive into the tax aspects of maintenance and repairs next chapter. During this chapter we are going to review the day to day actions required to keep an investment property profitable.

Repairs, Maintenance and Improvements

Before exploring what it takes to keep up real estate investments, it is first important to understand the difference between repairs, maintenance and improvements. The irs.gov website provides the complex tax code definitions and we'll dive deeper into taxes next chapter, but for now let's look at the basics for keeping up an investment.

Maintenance are any actions performed to keep the property clean, safe and livable for the tenants. This can include lawn and landscaping maintenance, replacing HVAC, refrigerator or other filters and even replacing lightbulbs. Some maintenance will be covered by the tenant and some are the responsibility of the owner. It is important to spell this out clearly in the lease. For instance, we like our properties to have refrigerators with in the door ice / water dispensers but we specify the tenant must replace the filters periodically. Of course when we reset a property, I'll throw a new filter in and count the cost as a maintenance expense.

Similarly, light bulbs are the tenant's responsibility with one caveat, any lighting (such as large fluorescent bulbs) that the tenant is incapable or uncomfortable replacing, I'll change out (and write off the expense). Lawn care is the responsibility of the tenant but I will trim the shrubs and replace mulch annually at our expense. HVAC filters are the responsibility of the tenant and this is one that is important to enforce.

Visually inspecting the roof for damages to shingles, sealing around windows and doors are examples of other regular maintenance tasks that I as the owner routinely perform. Quarterly pest control is another maintenance item that I cover for the properties that we manage. You get the idea! It is completely up to the owner how much maintenance of the home they want to entrust to the tenant, what they want to outsource and how much they want to take on. It is getting more common, especially for the larger apartment complexes, for 100% of the maintenance performed by property management. Worth considering when deciding how much to ask of the tenant.

So how does an owner make regular checks and perform maintenance to ensure the investment is being cared for without intruding on a tenant's right to privacy? First, if I go out to a property on a repair call I will make it a point to check several items when I am inside the property. Are the windows, screens and blinds serviceable? Any leaks under the sinks, holes in the wall or other items? Probably most importantly, is there a good filter in the HVAC. This goes for the exterior as well. I will walk around the property and make a visual inspection of the roof and windows. I make it a point to keep a stock of common maintenance items such as filters, caulk and bulbs on my truck. If upon an inspection of the roof any shingles look questionable, I will get it fixed before it becomes an issue.

One absolutely critical check is the leak test. Many people don't realize you can observe a home's water meter to determine if there are any leaks at least on the supply side (drains must be visually inspected). I will flip open the water meter lid every time I stop by a property and observe at least two to three minutes for movement on the meter.

These checks are the essence of maintenance. In the Army we called it Preventive Maintenance Checks and Services or PMCS. In the manual for any piece of equipment in the Army, there was a detailed list of PMCS checks to make. Perhaps there is a lesson to take away here! I've never gone so far as to make a checklist but it certainly is not a bad idea. While the tenants may get a bit annoyed at the checks, they will also appreciate that you are maintaining their home. And as we've already discussed often times they will mirror that behavior right back at you by calling immediately whenever there is a maintenance concern.

Sometimes the lines begin to blur when we start to talk repairs. Is painting a wall a repair or maintenance? Well if you consider patching holes in the wall and covering scuffed paint, it is definitely a repair! The same logic can be applied to flooring. Frayed and soiled carpets need to be repaired (or replaced as the case may be). Which leads me to an important point on repairs.

Oftentimes repair really means replace. I learned early on spending $400 to repair a 10 year old refrigerator is usually a losing proposition. Same with HVACs. That $1000 fan motor is usually a waste on a 15 year old unit. This is where the investor can really leverage the tax advantages of rental properties. Say that 12 year old refrigerator, the old fashioned kind, finally bit the dust. Definitely not worth repair. Additionally, the original stove and dishwasher are also on their last leg. It may be time to "repair" all three with brand new stainless steel models. Range fan hood stop working? Repair / replace with a modern stainless steel, over the range microwave!

While this might be an outlay in the near term, new appliances are one of the best repairs to make on a property as they will make the residence show better and demand higher rent. Best of all, these can be written off on taxes as repairs! Flooring, countertops, light fixtures and windows when they are no longer serviceable are all "repairs" that can increase the profitability of an investment and offer a tax advantage. You'd be surprised how replacing that broken down Formica countertop with granite, although pricey in the near term, will help a home rent or sell! There are some nuances to this which we'll cover in detail next chapter on taxes.

Finally, a word on improvements. Improvements are NOT tax deductible so the return on investment for an improvement must be considered carefully before committing the funds. What is an improvement? Adding an extra room, building a deck or porch, perhaps building a privacy fence for the back yard are all examples of improvements that may increase the value of the property and rents, but are not deductible from gross income according to the IRS.

I've only scratched the surface on repairs, maintenance and improvements. At the end of the day, one is only limited by their imagination, funding and physics. Equally important as knowing what to maintain and repair is knowing...

When to Repair and Maintain

First the obvious. Never walk past a serious maintenance issue and above all, ensure you are providing tenants a safe, clean, serviceable home. They are paying a lot of their hard earned money to live in a good home. Do not betray their trust by ignoring maintenance problems. There may be a very few occasions when it just makes more sense to defer a maintenance item until a tenant moves out based on the scope of the repair. I've found this is the exception more than the rule. It's just best practice to address maintenance issues immediately. Not only is it the right thing to do, your tenants will appreciate you for it and take it into consideration when it comes lease renewal time!

What is meant by deferred repairs or maintenance? We have a refrigerator in one unit that the ice dispenser is inoperable. It still makes ice, it just won't come out the door.

It would cost several hundred dollars to repair and the fridge is nearing the 10 year mark. We informed the tenants when they moved in of the issue with the promise that we will replace the fridge with a top of the line new one when it gives out. Flooring and paint are other examples. Unless there is a safety issue such as a trip hazard it is usually best to wait until the unit is empty before replacing flooring or repainting.

One item to consider on the "when" is supply chain and availability of contractors. Nowadays there are extremely long lead times on just about everything. We recently had a 20 year old duplex in dire need of new windows. There was a six month wait from the factory! No way to schedule major repairs like this for when the unit is empty. While the tenants were a bit inconvenienced during the two days it took to get their new windows installed, they really loved them when the job was done. The point is plan ahead and keep abreast on the availability of goods and services in your area. Finally, try to "market time" as much as possible. If you know there will be a need for an appliance within six months it may be wise to take advantage of that great Labor Day sale at the big box store.

The same goes for contractors. Other than plumbers and electricians who are still relatively responsive, if you need to make large repairs such as countertops, paint or even flooring, you may have to wait a few weeks until the installer's schedule clears up. We saw this time and again when we were building our new duplex investment.

Let me go back to the first paragraph in this section for a moment as that is truly the point of when to perform repairs. I already shared one example of how not getting a proper home inspection and making necessary repairs cost us time and money when a substandard supply line to a dishwasher gave out. Let me share another example of turning a blind eye to a needed repair…

In 2016 we found an excellent for sale by owner duplex at a great price. While there were some evident repair issues that would need to be addressed, at that price point, it was just too good of a deal to pass up. The most serious problem I noticed on the property was the location of the water meters. For whatever reason, the builders had placed the meters almost in the middle of the asphalt parking area with the water supplies to the units running under the asphalt.

It doesn't take an engineer to realize that vehicle traffic continually running over and sometimes parking on top of the concrete casements surrounding the water meters could put pressure on the PVC water supply lines and they would eventually crack. There was even visual evidence where a failure had already occurred and the lines had to be dug up, repaired and then the parking area repaved.

The obvious quick fix was to relocate the meters in a grassy area off the parking lot and reroute the water supply lines back into the building where they were not under asphalt and constantly exposed to vehicular traffic. This would take some time and a few thousand dollars to repair but overall, not the most complex job for skilled workers.

Of course, the point of this vignette is to illustrate why one should never walk past a maintenance or repair issue! For whatever reason (really no good excuse), I didn't make the required repairs after we closed on the property. Not six months later I got the call, on a long, Memorial Day weekend of course, that water was pooling up in the parking area. Sure enough, the water line was cracked at the meter due to the constant strain from vehicles driving over it!

Nothing better than a Memorial Day weekend spent busting asphalt with a pick axe and covered in mud to focus the mind! A handy man friend of mine helped me dig up, fix the water line and re asphalt the parking area on the cheap but I had blown a whole weekend and spent about $500. Worse yet, we had only made a temporary fix, the root cause of the problem wasn't resolved. A few months later I forked out the $3000 and assembled the professional help I needed to move the meters and reroute the supplies to the house fixing the problem properly. Haven't had to worry about it again.

So the short answer for "when" to perform repairs and maintenance is immediately if it is serious or a safety issue and defer only in limited circumstances when it would be more convenient for your tenants.

Learn How to do it yourself

To be a successful real estate investor, do it yourself skills are a must. Replacing a flush valve (the guts inside a toilet tank) is a relatively simple job that takes about $10 in parts and 15 minutes of time, but a plumber will charge around $100. Similarly, once the prep work is complete, slapping on a coat of paint is pretty easy. Installing blinds, light fixtures and basic plumbing are simple tasks the layperson can perform after watching a few videos on the internet. As for yard work and move out cleaning? Don't even think about hiring it out!

The bottom line is if an investor outsources every single maintenance, cleaning and repair job, it may be challenging to stay profitable on real estate investments. There are enough major repairs for a property such as water heaters and HVAC systems where an expert will have to be called in. This is why I get a kick out of the term "passive" income. Actively managing and maintaining rental properties is anything but passive. It is a bona fide part time job!

We budget a portion of our gross rental income monthly, currently $75 per unit per month, for anticipated repairs. Some years we will end up with a surplus- 2018 and 2020 were relatively worry free, 2019 was a nightmare! 2021 was another big spending year on maintenance. We replaced three HVAC units, windows on one of our buildings and some other fairly significant repairs!

While I complete the majority of the routine repairs myself, many of the issues we've encountered were well beyond my abilities. Last year we had to call in professionals, a lot more than usual! There are a lot of factors that go into whether to call in a professional or do it yourself. The nightmare scenario is to dig into a plumbing or electrical job only to realize it is beyond your ability half way through the job. This could mean leaving the tenant without water until an expert can arrive to fix your mess! Let me provide a recent example of where I erred on the side of caution on what on the surface seemed to be a really small repair.

Last year one of our properties had a leaking exterior hose bib. I've replace probably three or four of these in the past, not the most challenging plumbing job. But this one was positioned where the water supply had to be accessed from the interior of the home by cutting through drywall. Additionally, the water supplies in the house are PEX not PVC. I don't have a lot of experience working with PEX and it is a little trickier than PVC. I just didn't feel comfortable taking on the job. I called a plumber and about 30 minutes and $268 later it was fixed. If I had done it myself it would have cost about $10 in parts and a few hours on the weekend. The risk however could have been a catastrophic mess if I screwed it up. It just wasn't worth it.

I was however, able to save some money on a portion of the repair by doing it myself. While the plumber was able to quickly identify where the drywall needed to be cut and replace the hose bib, plumbers don't do drywall repair! I patched, sanded and painted the roughly 12in square opening in the wall myself at a cost of about $20. I am sure a handyman would have charged at least $100 making the total cost of a relatively small repair well over $300!

While I am not a do it yourself ninja, I've developed some skills over the years. In my humble opinion, I think developing do it yourself skills is a requirement for the successful real estate investor. My sons and I have cut grass, repaired drywall, rolled on paint, cleaned and generally fixed a lot in 2021. If we had outsourced all that work, I shudder to think how much we'd be overrun on our maintenance budget! These are just a few examples where we make our maintenance budget go further by doing it yourself. Bottom line, it will be a challenge to remain profitable in rentals if one continually pays others to perform common repairs.

I am consistently amazed by the number of folks who do not know how or are reluctant to perform the most basic home repairs and maintenance! Growing up in the country where resources were limited, I would help my family perform all but the most serious of home repairs. I guess you could say it is in my DNA to do it myself! Plumbers, electricians, painters and other skilled workers charge an arm and a leg for their time. Rightfully so, they have the skills and tools to make the tough jobs quick and simple. When doing it yourself, it will likely be neither quick nor simple.

Calling plumbers to replace leaky toilet flush valves, lawn care folks to trim the shrubs or painters to roll on a coat of paint is simply throwing money away. Over time the money saved doing it yourself is substantial and critical to sustaining a rental property business. The savings can be reinvested into new properties!

"But I am not mechanically inclined." That's ok, I am not either. I can't run a bead of caulk perfectly to save my life. But you know what, I can do it well enough! For all my concerns about today's interconnected, digital world, one outstanding advantage it gives us is a means to learn quickly. There are literally thousands of easy to follow, professionally produced, how-to videos on the internet with step by step instructions on how to perform most home repairs. Obvious implied task is possessing a smartphone good enough that, when wedged under a kitchen sink replacing a valve, you can see / hear the instructions!

Most of the common day to day home repair tasks are not analogous to brain surgery. With a 10 minute video, a few practice tries and the right safety measures in place, most common repairs can be performed safely and effectively by the layperson. When I do have to call in a professional for the tougher jobs, I always follow them closely and watch what they are doing. I always ask first before shadowing a plumber or electrician, but many are eager to show off their craft. I have learned more about plumbing and electrical repair this way and saved untold repair costs!

As a side note, plumbers and electricians clearly recognize they will lose work if by watching them, a customer learns how to do it themselves. I've found many professionals prefer this. Skilled professionals rather spend time on the higher paying, big jobs rather than the smaller ones that suck up their time.

Experience is the best teacher and yes there is some risk involved with doing it yourself. A 110 volt live wire does get your attention when it arcs. Rest assured, you will only forget to turn off power at the breaker box once! The key to doing it yourself is move slowly and deliberately. Calculate and understand each step. Do it yourself repair jobs will take two or three times longer than a pro, but it will save so much money. Eventually, after performing a repair several times, the do it yourselfer may even go as fast as a pro!

Many people are unwilling to trade their Saturday afternoon for wallowing around in the floor to fix a leaky pipe. But I assert it is absolutely necessary in order to turn a profit with rentals. This is simply part of the commitment we talked about in chapter one!

Knowing Who to Call

I closed the last chapter offering that if the people aspect of managing a property appears too much, then a property management company may be an option if the math on the investment works out. In principle, this also holds true for hiring out maintenance and repairs, but I just don't think it wise to pay others to do things one can do themselves. Nevertheless, calling in a pro will be required from time to time. As I've grown older, my general body condition and available time seem to be diminishing, I've found myself calling in more repairs than I used to. Critical to making this work is establishing a relationship with good vendors who are trustworthy and work reasonably.

What do I look for in a service provider or repair person? First and foremost for me is will the person pick up the phone when I call. Often, I've reached out to vendors who either would return my call two days later or sometimes not at all. Additionally, I've had plumbers, painters and electricians blow off or reschedule appointments at the last minute. This is an incredible inconvenience not only to me but also the tenant who may be waiting to let the worker in.

My number one criteria in establishing a relationship with a provider is they answer the phone on the first or second ring and come out to do the job when they say they will. Perhaps it is a sign of the times but these are increasingly more scarce attributes these days. Cost and quality of service are also paramount, but time in my opinion, is the most important factor.

Usually this level of service is more expensive. Oftentimes, these vendors may be the larger service providers with a full staff including a receptionist and dispatcher. Maybe the guy or gal down the street that moonlights as a handyman or licensed plumber may work cheaper. But my experience has shown it is much harder to get these folks scheduled quickly. I am willing to pay a little extra if we can get the repairs done correctly but also quickly.

All of that being said, don't throw away the number for the handyman down the street! The plumbers, electricians and handymen with the big office are definitely the go to for the repairs when there is an angry tenant with a leak in the ceiling. But what about when you have a little more time to plan a project?

I shared the story of our water damage fiasco in one of our condo units earlier. I'll provide a few more details of this vignette which shows why "knowing who to call" can save the investor money. Working with my insurance company on this claim was a near daily battle. At one point they threatened not to pay the claim! After raising some serious complaint, they finally said they would commit $10k for repairs. I called a general contractor to come take a look at the job and he laughed. He said he wouldn't touch the job for less than $30k.

Fortunately, I knew enough people in the area to serve as general contractor myself. A handyman friend did the drywall and trim. I did the paint. I caught cabinets and appliances on sale at the big box and there is a discount flooring store nearby I've done a lot of business with who cut me a deal. Bottom line, we got a brand new kitchen in the unit complete with flooring, cabinets, granite counter tops and stainless steel appliances for exactly $10k.

The moral of the story is knowing who to call. We maintain a pretty expansive "preferred vendor" spreadsheet and keep the contact info updated. This is an absolutely critical tool in the rental property business! Repairs will happen and sometimes you don't have a choice to do it yourself. Know who to call!

Everything I've just described regarding maintaining an investment I learned through 14 years of experience...and I still am learning every day! I've screwed it up plenty of times and learned from my mistakes. On that point, it is important to emphasize that the rental property investor must continually seek knowledge. Yet another very necessary time suck for the rental investor!

Whether learning how to replace a flush valve in a toilet or doing research on the best plumber in your area, continually seeking knowledge is a critical attribute for the rental property investor. This may mean less hours in front of the TV at night and more nights doing internet research on which big box has the best deal on a new stove for one of your units. Another example of the commitment required to own and manage rental properties.

Of course, going through a property management company can relieve the burden of maintaining a property. I've been very pleased with the repair vendors our property management company uses. They work quickly and don't gouge their rates. Also, our property management company sends very detailed inspections with literally hundreds of pictures. Enough for me to make an accurate assessment as to the condition of a property from 900 miles away. But all this comes at a cost. Whether maintaining yourself, hiring a repair person or relying completely on a property management company, maintaining the investments is a big part of the calculus the prospective investor must complete before diving into this wonderful business!

It's time to move on to another important task to maintain real estate investments. While not as physically demanding as wallowing under a sink to fix some plumbing, it is every bit as demanding of one's time. What am I talking about? Keeping the books and paying taxes of course!

Chapter 6: Bookkeeping and Taxes

If you've taken anything away from the last three chapters, owning and managing rental properties is work! Well this chapter adds to the challenge. So much for the so called "passive" income! Fortunately, this type of work is a lot less physically demanding than fixing a leaky pipe on a Saturday night. Record keeping is absolutely critical to good rental property investing. It is the only way to quantifiably measure the performance of your investment. With a rental property investment, it is the investor's responsibility to put together those fancy statements like those received form brokers on traditional investments! Of course, you can pay a property management company to provide detailed records, but that service doesn't come cheap!

Good data becomes good knowledge which informs good decisions. While there is truth in the adage the money in real estate is made when the property is purchased, if rents and expenses aren't carefully monitored and actively managed, the investment will underperform. My assumption is this is why some real estate investors may divest of their holdings earlier than anticipated. Additionally, impeccable records are required in order to take advantage of all the tax breaks rental investments offer. Fortunately, the bookkeeping and math skills required to collect and organize this data are not terribly hard. Anyone can do it, I am living proof of that! Additionally, there are some great software and online tools available to help if needed.

Before diving in to taxes let's look at the information a rental property investor needs to retain, organize and analyze to keep their investment profitable. "Bookkeeping" is not an ugly word!

Financials

There is a lot of great software to help rental property investors manage their portfolio. I have tried the name brand software, but honestly it's just not a good fit for me. I've found the time it takes to input properties and update information within the program's database is more than I want to spend behind the computer. So I use the old reliable, an Excel spreadsheet, to track our portfolio. It is easier to keep updated than the software and very easily tailorable. With a few simple formulas, the spreadsheet provides us the data we need to make informed decisions about our investment. I'm sure an Excel wizard could do even more! I back up the spreadsheet every month, renaming the file on the date I back it up.

Before diving into our home grown rental property financial management tool, a quick word on one of our key business practices. We use automatic payments for absolutely everything! There is seldom a time when I mail a check. Rather, we just monitor our bank and credit card's activity online to ensure payments are flowing in and out as they should. We have all the functionality we need using their online sites and smartphone apps; no need for any of these extra management tools or payment services I keep hearing so much about. We haven't had any major issues using this practice, but to clarify when I say monitor, I do mean daily, often several times a day. The very few times there has been an issue with a payment, we resolved the problem quickly.

Which brings us to the financial spreadsheet we use to track both the income and outgo on our properties as well as to track our equity. This is our primary tool to monitor performance of our investments. This is not the micro level ledger we use to track daily expenses. We will explore that

	Financials as of 22 May 20								
	Unit	Gross	P&I	Tax	Ins	HOA/Util	Mang.	Maint	tot exp	Net
1	123 Street, Anytown, US	800	0	65	52	220	0	50	387	413
2	130 Street, Anytown, US	830	0	59	61	220	0	50	390	440
3	142 Street, Anytown, US	820	0	63	51	228	0	50	392	428
4	150A Street, Anytown, US	825	237	49	35	25	0	50	396	429
5	150B Street, Anytown, US	825	237	49	35	0	0	50	371	454
6	160A Street, Anytown, US	830	341	52	34	0	0	50	477	353
7	160B Street, Anytown, US	820	341	52	34	0	0	50	477	343
8	170A Street, Anytown, US	820	350	52	35	0	0	50	487	333
9	170B Street, Anytown, US	820	350	52	35	0	0	50	487	333
Month		7390	1856	493	372	693	0	450	3864	3526
Annual		88680	22272	5916	4464	8316	0	5400	46368	42312

tool next. First let's look at a notional example of the income and outgo financials spreadsheet.

We track by unit rather than by building but it is easy enough to determine how a building is performing. Note, we will split the costs that apply to the building (such as principle and interest for the mortgage) between both units. Gross rent is simply what it sounds like, what the tenant pays us each month. P & I is the principle and interest on the loan (if applicable). For our property taxes, we "waive escrow" when we close and pay the taxes on our own. There are some advantages, one of which you see here is cleaner bookkeeping. I'll share other reasons why waiving escrow is a good idea in the next chapter on growing the business.

HOA / Utilities are the HOA fees and any utilities we may pay on behalf of the tenant per the lease. As a rule we don't include utilities but you can see here an example of where we did pay the water bill for one of our units a few years ago. There are a bunch of zeros in the management column but obviously for our properties in Texas, this column is populated, again broken out by unit. Lastly we see the maintenance column. This is what we budget for maintenance withhold each month per unit. Today, we withhold $75 per unit due to the rising cost of labor and materials. Note these funds do not go into any special account but maintenance

MUST be budgeted each month as we discussed at length last chapter! In the example above you see we budget $450 per month or $5400 per year. As we discussed in the last chapter, some years you won't spend near that much. Other years, you may replace two HVACs which will cost about $10000! We've found this dollar cost averaging budget method to work, but again key is knowing the condition of your property from the outset.

Some simple formulas add up the expenses and subtract from the gross providing the net income per unit each month. Totals are along the bottom for each category. I also like to average the net income (again another simple formula). When we first started our goal was to net $300 per unit. Not exactly sure where that number came from, but my logic was pocketing $300 per unit per month would make the business worth our time. You can see in this example the average exceeds our 2008 goal!

According to this example, net income is $3536 per month or a little over $42000 per year. This is nine units, three of which are single family condos and six are duplex units (three properties). We haven't even started talking yet about how the tax advantages of rental properties make that $42000 "feel" like more or how the equity is building! This is also an example based on a few years back. All of our rents have increased by over $100 per month in the past two years. Not to mention, we own a few more than nine units… Not too shabby for a side hustle!

A few final word on the financials spreadsheet. I also keep a "working" spreadsheet where I can plug in new rents, new properties and let the formulas spit out how that impacts the bottom line. It is always fun to dream. It is critical to keep the spreadsheet updated and review it often. Insurance premiums, taxes and maintenance all increase yearly.

We also maintain another spreadsheet called "rental rolls" which has tenant contact information, monthly rent, lease summary, deposits and any important notes. The rental rolls are useful tool to keep track of leases at a glance. The rental rolls spreadsheet complements the paper and digital

Equity As of May 20					
Basis	2020 Tax Val	Mortgage	Equity	Lender	Loan #
42000	67000	0	67000		
51000	60000	0	60000		
53000	70900	0	70900		
135000	168100	89500	78600	First Bank	92131572
173000	177200	116822	60378	First Bank	108025404
173000	176800	122076	54724	Amerihome	112909098
627000	720000	328398	391602		

copies we maintain of lease agreements, addendums and any other business paperwork. Now that we've looked at the financials spreadsheet, let's look at the equity portion.

The data above would actually be located just to the right of the financials, however, I couldn't get it all to fit on the page of this book! Some may consider tracking equity as "counting your money while you are sitting at the table" to borrow a line from an old song but I think it is important to monitor how equity is growing. Not only does this make the real estate investor aware of equity available for possible creative financing opportunities, the investor will need positive affirmations on why they made this sometimes time consuming commitment!

Starting from the left, basis is what it cost to put the property into operation. This will be the purchase price, closing fees and any repairs. We will talk more about basis and how it is used to calculate depreciation later in the tax portion. The next column is tax value. This is what I use to determine the current value of the property. Tax values are generally lower than market values but again I like to figure conservatively. Just using the first property on this spreadsheet, the tax value is $67000 but I am highly confident it would sell (probably within hours) for at least $100000 if listed on the market today. Market values can be placed in this column if desired, there are a lot of good websites which provide home value monitoring services. Important to remember, market value is a moving target!

The next column is mortgage or how much is owed on the property. Note the three condos are owned outright, we reviewed earlier some creative financing options that helped us pick up these condos with no long term debt. And finally the good part, equity. Equity is simply the difference between what the property is worth and what is owed on it. You can see by this example, about $391K total in equity! So what is that in actual ROI?

This is just an example but for arguments sake let's assume all of these properties were acquired within five years of the spreadsheet's creation at a total initial investment of about $200k. As discussed, while some of that $200k down may have come from income earned at a day job, it can also come from other rentals or mutual fund investment income. Regardless, that $200k down grew to nearly double in just five years! Again, this is figuring conservatively, market values are much higher than tax values, the actual equity could be much more. Not a bad ROI! Someone handy with Excel could very easily add columns and formulas that would provide other data points or even spit out fancy graphs as desired.

I can't stress enough keeping the data updated in these spreadsheets (or property management software) is absolutely critical. I probably look at these spreadsheets a minimum of weekly but often times several times a week. Neglect the numbers for several months and an investor may find the investment has lost $10k or more in profit that it didn't need to! What I have just covered is the easy part of rental property bookkeeping, now on to the day to day grind of bookkeeping work!

Maintain Receipts and a Ledger

In order to take advantage of the many tax benefits of rental property investing, the owner must maintain detailed records of every expense. This will make tax time a snap and also keep the owner out of trouble in the event of an audit. Just like for property management, there are a lot of great software and apps on the market that can help an owner keep track of expenses. Some credit card apps even have great receipt management features that I've used in the past. But, what I've found most effective to maintain expenses is, you guessed it, an Excel spreadsheet!

Before we dive into the ledger, let's talk about maintaining receipts. Again, many folks keep everything digital to include scanning paper receipts but I've just found scanning paper copies takes more time than I want to spend. I maintain an "accordion" file folder tabbed by unit. When I have an expense, I bring the receipt home (this is sometime harder than it sounds), log the expense on the Excel spreadsheet ledger and place the receipt into the file for the unit. Important to note for tax purposes, expenses are tracked by building, not unit, but I still like to keep it broke down by unit for good bookkeeping purposes. When it is time to do taxes, I remove the receipts from the accordion file folder and reconcile one last time with the ledger spreadsheet. Bam, you're done!

There will sometimes be digital only receipts such as for property taxes, insurance premiums and online material purchases. I simply record the expense on our ledger and save the digital receipt in a well-marked file folder on our PC. Coming up in the portion on taxes I'll talk briefly about mileage expenses as they are tracked slightly differently for tax purposes.

Maintaining the receipt is the key part. If an owner doesn't have proof of an expense they simply can't deduct it on their taxes. But organization is key. Keeping receipts jumbled up in a shoe box may be almost as ineffective as not maintaining the receipt at all! Maintaining these records for posterity is important. We have a cloud backup service that backs up all of our business files. Yet another deductible expense!

To make sense of it all, the owner must maintain a ledger. Below is a snapshot example from the type of Excel spread sheet we use for our ledger. Note this is 30 entries for a month's time; in a typical year, there are over 300 entries!

Like most things, I keep it simple. Obviously the location column has the property address and the payee column contains the tenant's last name, I've deleted that data for privacy. This also makes the data sortable. With a few simple clicks you can sort to determine how much has been spent by type of expense on a certain property or a tenants particular payment habits.

We back up this data every month. Note there are a couple of expenses not reflected on this ledger. I don't include HOA fees as well as mortgage principle and interest as those

Entry	Date	Location	Payee	Description	Details	Amount
				2021 Ledger		
1	12/16/2021	Address	Owner	2021 Property Taxes		($1,275.12)
2	12/26/2021	Address	Owner	Repairs	Lowes Caulk	($7.43)
3	12/20/2021	Address	Owner	Tenant Screening	Transunion Smart move	($30.00)
4	12/17/2021	unassigned	Owner	Office supplies	Printer toner	($43.15)
5	12/16/2021	unassigned	Owner	Tax transaction fee		($101.01)
6	12/16/2021	Address	Owner	2021 Property Taxes		($1,378.38)
7	12/16/2021	Address	Owner	2021 Property Taxes		($1,374.73)
8	12/15/2021	Address	Tenant	Rent	Paid partial month July; late fee; SVDP	$550.00
9	12/15/2021	Address	Owner	Tenant Screening	Transunion Smart move X1	($30.00)
10	12/15/2021	Address	Tenant	Rent	December + Late Fee	$950.00
11	12/13/2021	unassigned	Owner	Office supplies	USPS stamps	($11.60)
12	12/13/2021	Address	Owner	Tenant Screening	TU smartmove X3 apps	($120.00)
13	12/12/2021	Address	Owner	Repairs	Bulbs	($20.12)
14	12/10/2021	Address	Owner	Advertising	Zillow	($9.99)
15	12/9/2021	Address	Tenant	Rent	Late Fee	$850.00
16	12/8/2021	Address	Tenant	Rent	Late Fee	$860.00
17	12/8/2021	unassigned	Owner	Business	Storage	($39.00)
18	12/5/2021	Address	Owner	Repairs	Lowes replace blinds	($204.83)
19	12/5/2021	Address	Tenant	Rent		$820.00
20	12/5/2021	Address	Tenant	Rent		$950.00
21	12/5/2021	Address	Tenant	Rent		$850.00
22	12/5/2021	Address	Tenant	Rent		$820.00
23	12/5/2021	Address	Tenant	Rent		$825.00
24	12/4/2021	unassigned	Owner	Holiday Gift Cards	Walmart gift cards $25 X 9	($226.07)
25	12/4/2021	unassigned	Owner	Office supplies	Stamps	($11.60)
26	12/4/2021	Address	Owner	Repairs	Refrigerator filter	($51.97)
27	11/22/2021	Address	Owner	2021 Property Taxes	Visa	($974.20)
28	11/22/2021	Address	Owner	2021 Property Taxes	Visa	($42.88)
29	11/22/2021	Address	Owner	2021 Property Taxes	Visa	($943.51)
30	11/22/2021	Address	Owner	2021 Property Taxes	Visa	($854.38)
31	11/22/2021	Address	Owner	Tax transaction fee	Visa	($70.68)

payments are set up automatically from our business account but it would be easy enough to add both if desired. This ledger also is only for our local properties that we actively manage. The rental property management company who handles our Texas properties has a very similar ledger easily downloadable in excel format. Where do you think I got the format?

As mentioned, come tax time, I pull the receipts out of the accordion file and reconcile with this ledger. There may be one or two corrections required to make the ledger and receipts reconcile. Upon completion, I store the receipts for posterity in a letter sized envelope writing the property name and expenses by type on the outside. Digital items are backed up in a structured file system to both our home external drive and cloud storage. We do our own taxes, more on that in just a moment, but I think even if I hired an accountant, this system would be readily accepted and make their job easier.

While it takes some discipline to maintain receipts, log the item and properly store the receipt for every expense, these simple tasks must become second nature. If not, the consequences could be severe to include profit loss, a real headache around tax time and absolutely worse case, a bad IRS audit outcome. Speaking of the IRS, let's move on to one of my favorite topics...

Leveraging the Tax Benefits of Real Estate

Whether deeded in the name of a LLC or the owner's name, rental property income is accounted for on a personal income tax return. It is considered passive income. This in itself is an advantage of real estate investing as business or corporate tax can get complex. While rental property taxes are pretty straight forward, before investing, I highly recommend consulting a tax professional or using tax software designed for rental property owners to learn more. We use tax software and have not had any issues.

At the very basic level, the tax paid on rental property income is based on the difference between the gross collected rent and the expense to operate and maintain the property as a rental. This is where it gets exciting! The scope of these expenses is fairly broad. This is one distinct advantage real estate investments hold over traditional market based investments. Most people can't write off investment account expenses anymore. Additionally, and this is the best part, the IRS has some unique rules for determining what constitutes an expense.

Repairs, maintenance and cleaning are pretty straight forward. If paying someone to fix a leaky faucet or clean a property, the cost of the bill is deducted from the gross income. Similarly, if the owner makes the repairs, the cost of the materials for the repair as well as in some cases even the tools are deducted. If repairs are major, generally defined as costing more than $2500, such as replacing an HVAC, roof or new windows, then the repair becomes real property that can be depreciated over time (more on depreciation coming up).

Cleaning supplies, a box of nails, a gallon of paint or a bag of grass seeds are all examples of materials which are commonly deducted as expenses to maintain or repair a rental property. One may ask, well how does the IRS know if I use all of the cleaning product on the rental property? Only the cost of the materials that are used for the rental property are supposed to be deducted….and that is all I am going to say on this point!

Similarly, if one of the appliances craps out and it's time for a new one, the cost to replace that refrigerator, oven or dishwasher can be written off as a repair. As stated in the last chapter, this presents an excellent opportunity to upgrade to nicer appliances that will potentially help increase rents or resale values. The investor gets the benefit of putting some "sweat equity" into the property as well as a tax write off! A quick reminder, it is only repairs. While an owner can certainly add a deck or patio to a rental property, those are improvements and not deductible!

The other common deductions are what I call the price of doing business items. This includes insurance premiums, HOA dues, property taxes and my personal favorite, mortgage or business loan interest! There are some other price of doing business expenses that are also deductible but they must be directly related to owning and maintaining the rental property. This could include certain property management software, PO box fees, business taxes and other items or services needed to operate the rental. I've said it once, I'll say it again, check with a tax professional if any questions!

One expense I particularly love is mileage deductions. As of 2020 the IRS mileage deduction is .58 cents per mile. If a property is located on the route to work and the owner stops by to show, repair or otherwise manage the rental on their commute, then that portion of the route is deductible! Similarly, if making a trip to the local big box to pick up material for repairs or really any other rental related errand, those trips are deductible! What if I buy something else for personal use while I'm at the big box? Read between the lines!

Mileage expense adds up very quickly and I daresay it doesn't cost exactly .58 cents a mile to operate a vehicle. Planning business mileage wisely is an excellent way to realize the tax benefits of rental property ownership. That being said, the IRS does require well documented mileage reports for these trips. Thankfully there are some awesome smartphone apps that help manage the task. Just keep the app running in the back ground and it will capture all daily trips, then at the end of the day, review each trip and designate which ones were rental property related and which ones were personal. We've averaged over $2000 in deductions each year on business mileage! Below is an excerpt example of the IRS acceptable spreadsheet that our mileage app spits out.

SUMMARY							
VEHICLE	ODOMETER	BUSINESS	COMMUTE	PERSONAL (OTHER)	UNCLASSIFIED	TOTAL DISTANCE	MEDICAL
	0	4181	0	8812	0	12993	0
	TOTALS	4181	0	8812	0	12993	0

DETAILED LOG							
START_DATE*	END_DATE*	CATEGORY*	START*	STOP*	MILES*	MILES_VALUE	PURPOSE
1/5/2021 17:50	1/5/2021 18:12	Business	Location	Location	10.2	#REF!	Business
2/5/2021 8:55	2/5/2021 9:06	Business	Location	Location	2.3	#REF!	Business
2/5/2021 12:29	2/5/2021 12:39	Business	Location	Location	3.1	#REF!	Business
2/5/2021 17:03	2/5/2021 17:26	Business	Location	Location	4	#REF!	Business
2/5/2021 17:50	2/5/2021 18:19	Business	Location	Location	11.6	#REF!	Business
6/23/2021 16:45	6/23/2021 17:08	Business	Location	Location	9	#REF!	Business
6/23/2021 17:57	6/23/2021 18:14	Business	Location	Location	7	#REF!	Business
7/3/2021 11:21	7/3/2021 11:56	Business	Location	Location	8.6	#REF!	Business
7/3/2021 12:04	7/3/2021 12:25	Business	Location	Location	5.1	#REF!	Business
7/6/2021 10:06	7/6/2021 10:11	Business	Location	Location	9.9	#REF!	Business
7/6/2021 10:58	7/6/2021 11:04	Business	Location	Location	17.5	#REF!	Business
7/6/2021 13:39	7/6/2021 13:55	Business	Location	Location	9.6	#REF!	Business

Lastly, my favorite deduction from rental income is depreciation! Depreciation is simply reducing the value of a certain property over its useful life. Real estate, the structure only, can be depreciated over its useful life, a maximum of 27.5 years as currently determined by the IRS and can be depreciated all the way down to zero. The most common means for determining depreciation is the straight line method but again use an accountant or tax software to determine exact depreciation for each tax year. To determine depreciation one must know the cost basis for the property. Basis is what it cost to take ownership and place the property into operation.

Basis for the property can include many of the required fees to purchase the property as well as repairs required to get it rent ready. Let's say an investor bought a property for a purchase price of $140000 but with closing costs and some repairs, the final cost to get renters in the door was $150000. $150000 can be used as the cost basis as long as everything is documented. This will be the starting point for calculating annual depreciation over the next 27.5 years.

Using this same example and the straight line method, this property could be depreciated $5455 each year owned! The depreciation would be deducted from gross rental income for the property along with all the other expenses, greatly reducing taxable income or perhaps even creating an on paper loss. As mentioned earlier, real estate owners may also depreciate major repairs and even tools required to keep the property maintained. This gets a little complicated to keep up with and yet again a reason to secure a good tax software program or accountant.

Capital Gains Tax and Depreciation Recapture

Depreciation is the best tax benefit of owning investment property but it does come with a catch. You didn't think the IRS was going to let you keep all of that great benefit? When selling an investment property, the investor will have to pay capital gains taxes and depreciation recapture. Yet another reason, perhaps the primary reason, real estate is a long term investment!

First a look at capital gains using the numbers from the previous section. Let's say the seller held that property they purchased for $150000 for 10 years and sold it for a net of $200000 (after all seller costs and commissions are paid). There will be capital gains tax on the $50,000 profit. Capital gains tax are generally 15% but can run up to 20% depending on the gain. In this example, 15% would be a $7,500 capital gains tax bill.

Depreciation recapture is a little more complicated. Recapture is the IRS collecting income tax on the income offset (depreciation deduction) they gave you all those years. Depreciation recapture is taxed at the filer's personal income tax bracket. Sticking with the numbers we've used so far and assuming the investor is in the 22% tax bracket, after selling a property depreciated for 10 years at $5455 per year, the investor will have to pay $12000 in depreciation recapture tax. This means there is the potential for a total of $19500 in taxes when disposing of the property.

A $19500 tax bill on a $50000 profit is hefty to be sure. So isn't the tax break associated with rental property investing really a question of pay now or pay later? Perhaps, but I am a firm believer in the time value of money which in simplest terms means $1000 invested today is worth a whole lot more in 20 years than if one were to just hang on to it and wait 20 years before investing.

I've said it once, I'll say it a hundred times; rental properties are a long term investment. I used a 10 year example to show capital gains and depreciation recapture but what if the asset was held 15 years, 20 years or even longer? Each year the investor would receive that $5455 depreciation deduction on their personal taxes. The growth of 10-20 years' worth of tax advantaged income from real estate that is wisely reinvested should more than offset any tax burden when the property is eventually sold.

Also, there are a few tax advantaged means to dispose of a real estate investment. A 1031 exchange rolls the proceeds from the sale of a property towards the purchase of a like kind investment thus avoiding capital gains and depreciation recapture tax. How could this play out? Say you are getting to the stage in life where managing that duplex is too much hassle. Sell the duplex in a 1031 exchange and use the proceeds to buy a beachfront condo! As long as the primary purpose of the condo is as a rental, there will be no capital gains tax. The owner can still have some personal use of the condo, up to a point...again check with a tax professional.

Currently, passing on an investment property as part of an estate will also mitigate the tax burden if the heirs choose to sell the property. Simply put, one's heirs do not inherit the depreciation, the basis is reset. As of 2021 there is increasing discussion in the political arena about doing away with this benefit.

Regardless, even if a real estate investor sells an asset outright paying capital gains and depreciation recapture tax, the here and now tax advantages to owning real estate are substantial. The tax advantaged profit from rentals, wisely reinvested outweighs the tax burden. The tax bill an investor faces when disposing of an investment may be another reason some chose not to invest in real estate, but I hope I've shown the tax break in the here in now offset the bill. There are only two things certain in life, taxes are one of them. Income tax is not always a bad thing, after all it means the investor is making a profit!

Taxes in Practice

So what does all this tax business look like in practice? I'll provide some very general examples from our experience. After all the aforementioned expenses are deducted from our gross rental income, our *taxable rental income* is usually around 50% or less than what we actually net! Say we netted, put in our pockets, $30000 in a particular year. Due to the way expenses are calculated, we would expect to pay taxes as if the income was around $15000! Note these are just general assumptions. Everyone's tax situation is different but this provides an idea for planning. This tax advantage makes that $30000 in net income "feel" like a lot more.

Imagine how much one has to make to bring home $30000 net when their salary is subject to not only income tax but Medicare, social security tax and all the other deductions that hit our paychecks? All that being said, an investor still has to pay income taxes. How does one actually pay taxes on rental income without getting stuck with a huge tax bill upon filing an annual tax return?

To answer this question I will share my experiences with federal income tax as a rental property investor. One of the many benefits I encountered while serving in the military for 24 years was to remain blissfully ignorant about income taxes. Serving in the military presents some unique tax advantages due to the way service members are compensated. Even with additional income from real estate and mutual fund investing in taxable accounts, over the course of my career, our effective tax rate remained relatively low and we received a small refund every year.

As I transitioned out of the military and began civilian employment, I received a quick lesson on taxes in the real world! Naively, I claimed only myself and spouse on my federal tax W4 form when I began my civilian career. I left my two children off thinking that should allow for adequate withholding. Since I retired towards the end of 2019, I only received a few civilian employer paychecks but it was enough to make a surprising discovery when preparing our 2019 return!

I realized we were going to be severely under paid for tax year 2020. What I learned, and what I'm sure most civilians probably already knew, is that withholding is based on the compensation for that particular job. If the employee has other sources of income such as military retirement or passive income from real estate investments, they could very well be in a higher tax bracket! This is a good problem to have, but it must be prepared for.

About mid-year 2020 I adjusted my W4 so that my employer took out additional withhold to cover the taxes for the rental property income. Another option would have been to withhold at the single rate. Military retirees can also increase withhold from their retirement check if that's a better option. The IRS will also gladly accept anticipated tax payments at any time throughout the year. Important to note, if a taxpayer underpays in a given year they will not only face a huge tax bill come federal income tax time, they may also have to pay a fine! Thankfully, I caught this potential underpayment early and we came in just about even on our 2020 federal tax return, just the way I like it.

How does rental property income impact state income taxes? Again, let me share my experiences on the topic! Another tax "benefit" of military service is that service members can claim just about any state of residence while serving. I claimed my home state of Tennessee for 24 years. Tennessee is one of the few remaining states without an income tax. But when veterans retire from service, they usually must become legal residents of the state in which they will be working. The state we landed in has an income tax.

Based on a co-worker's recommendation, I claimed zero dependents on my state W4 so they would take out max withholding. Not going to lie, it stung a little bit seeing both federal and state income tax withholding going out every pay period! Thankfully, my new home state does not tax military retirement. As I prepared my 2020 state income tax return using a popular tax preparation software, I noticed many similarities to the federal return but also some distinct differences. One of the biggest differences is my state lets taxpayers "double dip" on investment property depreciation.

This simply means one can deduct depreciation of the investment property twice, once from the gross rental income on the property which reduces taxable income as we discussed earlier. Then again as an itemized deduction for the depreciation of an investment property. "Double dipping" on depreciation used to be the case on federal returns a few years ago and was a glorious thing! Unfortunately, federal tax law changed and depreciation of investment properties are now only deducted once on federal taxes.

Because my state still permits rental property depreciation double dipping, our itemized deductions were substantial which reduced state taxable income. Bottom line, it was just the opposite of my federal return and we over paid significantly on state income taxes! While we received a huge refund, my preference is to always come in "on time" when it comes to income taxes. I promptly adjusted my state W4 to reflect actual number of dependents in order to reduce state withholding each pay period. If I had just taken the time to talk to an accountant as I underwent a significant life change, we would have saved ourselves a lot of headache!

I know there was a lot of spreadsheets, numbers and tax talk in this chapter! As stated in chapter one, there are three ways an investor makes money on rental properties 1) net rental income 2) building equity 3) tax advantages. They are not mutually exclusive. Good bookkeeping and a solid understanding of personal income taxes are crucial to realizing all three of these potential sources for profit. I'll recap briefly.

There are two "books" to keep. First your portfolio financials spreadsheet which monitors, at the top level, monthly income and outgo. This is your monthly financial "statement" for your real estate investment portfolio. It is used to determine how your investment is performing and the financials spreadsheet will serve as the primary tool to make sound decisions about how to maximize the investments. Financials should also include a spreadsheet to track equity which is updated periodically, maybe even monthly. Unlike a taxable investment or retirement account, the real estate investor is responsible for making their own fancy statement each month!

The second "book" is the daily ledger and receipts. With 17 rental units, I am putting an entry into the ledger almost every day. Keeping a tight ledger with a traceable receipt either digital or paper is absolutely critical to taking advantage of the tax benefits of owning real estate.

If this all seems a bit overwhelming, then there are options. Again, property management companies will do a lot of the bookkeeping for you; in my opinion, this is the biggest reason they charge a 10% per month fee. Most keep very good records that can either be easily downloaded into the tax software of your choice or handed over to your accountant. Bottom line, property management companies prepare and hand over the "books" every year making this aspect of real estate investing much easier.

At tax time the benefit in the here and now is substantial. As an example, if you put $30000 from rental income in your pocket, the investor will most likely pay income tax for less. This is primarily due to how the IRS allows expenses and depreciation which are deducted from gross rental income. Depreciation is the best tax advantage of real estate investing but may be perceived by some as pay now or pay later. However, the tax benefit in the here in now, wisely reinvested far outweighs the capital gains and depreciation recapture tax burden when one finally disposes of an asset.

Oftentimes you see on social media or on television investors touting that they own "hundreds" of properties and make millions each year on real estate. Some will even add they started all of this with no money down. Usually these folks are trying to sell a book or seminar fee. In practice, it would take a large team of associates to help manage a portfolio of "hundreds" of properties. If in fact they are telling the truth, those investors are in a different league than my wife and I.

I hope the last few chapters have illustrated not only the commitment required to invest in real estate but also the tremendous benefits. My wife and I are in the "mom and pop" rental business. We grew our real estate investment from two units to seventeen in just about 14 years and have made our business in to a successful side hustle. That being said, we are at about the max we can handle in conjunction with my day job and our family commitments.

Which brings us to the next chapter, how does an investor grow from 2 to 17 or even 200 units? Read on, to find out!

Chapter 7: Grow and Secure your Business

I've said it once I've said it a hundred times, although the IRS considers rental income as passive on a personal return, the ownership and management of rental property is in practice, a part time business. Even if a property management company is handling the day to day, it should be clear by now that rental properties require near constant monitoring, decisions and action by the owners. For those rental property investors like my wife and I who have day jobs and a family, the challenge of keeping up a rental property side business is real.

Thankfully, my wife who has been a stay at home parent for most of our 21 years of marriage, takes a very active role in running our rental property business. Between the two of us we probably put in a minimum of 20 hours a week working on our business and often much more. It may be as simple as updating a spreadsheet or having a discussion about a tenant but there is always something.

So why grow? I outlined in the first two chapters a little about how we got into real estate investing and our goals. I recall thinking when we first started out it would be nice to end up with around a dozen units. By my fuzzy math, twelve units would give us flexibility for early retirement and other financial goals. We are currently at 17! I really can't offer the rationale or thought process on why we went from two units to seventeen in a little over a decade. I think it mostly may be due to the addictive nature of real estate investing. The excitement of selecting a new property and closing the deal is tremendous. Despite the occasional challenges, when the rent checks roll in it is a good feeling. Especially when there is a month with no maintenance expenses! Simply put, it is the best side business for our family. Right now the reward from rental property investing far outweighs the risk and sacrifice.

Check with me in about 10-15 years! We may have cashed out by then. Note there is not a chapter in this book about disposing of real estate as we haven't crossed that bridge yet and don't plan to for at least another decade. We've never sold a real estate investment! Right now we are very content with managing the 17 units we own and currently, aren't seeking to acquire anymore. But we still want to grow...

How's that work? Certainly growth can imply the acquisition of more properties. I shared earlier in the book how we grew our portfolio by investing the net income from our properties into taxable mutual funds and then using that growth to invest into other properties for the first dozen years. A snowball effect in simplest terms. We didn't even think for a second about taking a draw for over 10 years. But now we are taking draws and have decided to not pursue any more properties for the time being. How can we still grow our business?

Rental property investors can continue to grow the profitability of their portfolio by constantly creating efficiencies in almost every aspect of the operation. Additionally, part of growing is protecting against loss by adequately safeguarding the investment. The book keeping covered during the last chapter is the tool real estate investors must use to make good decisions on how to grow the investment.

That is the context for "growth" in this chapter. My apologies if you thought I was going to provide a step by step on how to go from purchasing duplexes to 100 unit apartment buildings! That is not my area of expertise, we are a "mom and pop" business. I have a feeling most investors are like us rather than the apartment building investors! That being said, most of the concepts we've covered in this book could easily be applied by those seeking to grow their real estate investment from side hustle to main hustle. Just skip the owner draws and reinvest your profits to buy more assets!

To Form a LLC or Not

First let's address the 400lb gorilla in the room. Should the real estate investor form a business, most typically a Limited Liability Corporation, or not? The short answer is yes. The benefits of doing business as an LLC far outweigh the additional costs and administrative burden for a number of reasons. Important to point out, for tax purposes, the profits from any real estate assets held in an LLC are handled just like any other real estate investment, on personal income taxes. This avoids the sometimes complicated and expensive corporate taxes incurred by an S Corporation or other entity.

Just as the name implies, a "Limited Liability Corporation" or LLC provides a layer of protection such that, in the event of a lawsuit, only the LLC's assets are potentially at risk, not the investor's personal assets. To title a property to an LLC, one will either need to purchase it with a business loan which has generally less favorable terms than a conventional mortgage or pay cash. The majority of our properties were purchased using conventional mortgages so therefore are titled in our own names. We did purchase three condo units via cash sales and titled those units in our LLC which as far as exposure goes, condo units are probably the most risky anyway.

Some investors take this level of protection to the extreme and will form a separate LLC or a "serial" LLC for every property they own. This would incur some pretty substantial attorney and business tax fees (all of which would be deductible) not to mention a lot of additional admin to maintain, but would offer the owner maximum protection of their personal assets.

We do business as an LLC, own some of our assets in the LLC and also have our LLC listed as additional insured on all of our rental properties. I am not 100% convinced forming an LLC solely for the additional layer of liability protection is absolutely necessary. Insurance provides a reasonable layer of protection which I'll dig into in just a moment. I think there are more compelling reasons for the amateur real estate investor to form an LLC.

For us, doing business as a business rather than as an individual is the number one reason for forming an LLC. An LLC will enable the real estate investor to establish business bank accounts, business credit cards and generally do all business related matters in the name of the LLC rather than in the investor's own name. This adds that layer of separation between an investor's personal finances and their business dealings. We established bank accounts, credit cards, PO Box, email accounts, google phone accounts etc... all in the name of our LLC. We don't use our personal emails, phones or of course mailing address in any of our business dealings. Although I am sure our personal information would be easy enough to find, it would require someone to actually go through the effort rather than just handing them the information.

As mentioned, the great thing about an LLC is that for tax purposes, income generated from the rental properties is just counted as regular individual income. No need to mess around with any of the confusing corporate tax mess! With an LLC, the real estate investor gets to enjoy the perks of being a business owner without the complicated taxes.

I was amazed at some of the opportunities available to businesses. Definitely a great resource for creative financing. Additionally, business accounts and credit cards come with a lot of additional perks. I'll briefly share one of my favorite life hacks we use both with our business accounts and personal credit card that has brought our family a lot of joy.

To earn your business, many credit cards offer some type of rewards in the form of cash back or are partnered with hotel / airline travel point programs. This creates an opportunity for a life hack that when managed properly, results in extra "income" in the form of free travel benefits or cash back. After some trial and error, we went with a major hotel chain for our personal card and an airline for our business card. The programs offer very generous points for purchases and several bonus opportunities based on spending. Additionally, when we signed up there was a large bonus point offer after the first few purchases.

While there are a lot of enticing benefits with rewards cards, important to remember many include an annual fee, but like most things, it is deductible from gross rental income! Hotels and airlines were the best fit for us but cash back (sometimes up to 3%) may be better for some. Having some free hotel nights or air fare can help make a periodic vacation a reality for the stressed out real estate investor!

We put every single purchase on our credit card and then pay it off every month. When I say every single purchase, I mean every single purchase. From a gallon of paint, to utility bill payments, property taxes, anything that a vendor will let us charge on a card. I will usually pay the convenience fees for purchases if not too outrageous. Most of the time these convenience fees are deductible (such as in the case for property taxes) but be sure to double check with a tax professional. As a result, our rewards points stack up quickly.

If executed correctly, this financial tactic is a fun little life hack that could reward the hard working real estate investor every year either in travel benefits or cash. We've paid for a lot of nice family vacations using points acquired from our rental property business. Also, paying off the card balance in its entirety every month reflects well on credit scores over time. I can't stress enough, paying off the bill every month is key for this little tactic to work!

We didn't establish an LLC until about eight years into our rental property investment adventure. There are fees required to establish an LLC and usually payment of annual business privilege taxes to maintain the entity (all tax deductible). Despite the additional costs, moving our real estate investments to an LLC was a good move for us.

Eventually, we will place the deeds for all of our properties in our LLC for the added layer of liability protection. Remember, there is no requirement for the real estate investor to form a business. In theory, an individual could own 100 rental properties in their own name and claim the passive income on their individual return for tax purposes. Consider the pros and cons to determine if establishing a LLC to hold real estate investments in is the right move for your personal situation.

Insuring the Investment

Probably a very good reason many people choose to not plunge into real estate investing is the very real risk that comes with owning property. What if the property burns down or is otherwise damaged? What if a tenant or their guest is injured at the property? Valid concerns, but fortunately there are several ways to protect ones interests from these infrequent occurrences. We just briefly covered LLCs as one means. Now let's dive into insurance.

Over the years in the real estate business, we've had a few issues. I'll go over some ways to "cover your assets" and share some of our scar tissue. Again, this is yet another area where more self-study is required to determine the best coverage plan for your personal situation. Most insurance companies offer rental property homeowners insurance that will offer the coverages required by not only the mortgage lender, but also state law. An owner can dial up or dial down coverages, deductibles and other features of these policies but with every change comes an associated cost in premiums. We choose to keep fairly high deductibles on our policies and only go with the minimum required coverages by law in order to keep annual premiums low. For the states where we own property, this includes rebuild cost in the case of a total loss as well as liability coverage for injury to tenants.

An important note, rental property homeowner's policies do not cover the renter's contents at the property. It is very important to explain this to tenants in the lease and highly recommend they secure a renters policy for the residence. I shared earlier that we require tenants to maintain a renters policy if they request to make any improvements (such as the addition of a trampoline) to the property. In this continuously litigious world we live in, we are considering making renter's policies mandatory for all of our tenants but haven't gone there yet.

Another feature rental property homeowner's policies include is lost rent coverage. This is an important feature that is usually set at 10% of the insured value. We had to use the lost rent clause in our policy when we had the massive water leak in one of our units that I shared earlier in the book. It just wasn't right to charge our tenant rent when the home was unlivable while undergoing repairs.

Rental property policies are not that different from a regular homeowner's policy but the investor should ensure a good understanding of coverages and costs. This is yet another part of the near continual calculus required to acquire and maintain rental investments. Often insurance companies will arbitrarily raise rebuild cost coverage every couple of years which results in a corresponding hike in premiums.

Monitor this closely! They will reduce the coverage (to an extent) just as quickly when you call them out. Don't over insure but absolutely do not under insure. Work with an insurance agency you trust to determine the right policy for your investment.

We have filed claims on our rental property homeowner's insurance policy twice. While both of these events caused some stress, in the long term, we came out on top and even increased the value of our properties! Our first claim was for a roof on one of our slightly older duplexes. It was beginning to have recurring leaks and a wind storm pretty much finished it off. This also was one of our out of state properties managed by a property manager.

Working with our insurance company and property management team, we were able to get a better, longer lasting, more attractive roof installed and we only paid the deductible on our policy. The deductible was able to be written off our taxes as a repair and the new roof certainly added value and curb appeal to the property. This process is pretty much automatic for the insurance companies and it went fairly smooth.

You've already heard about our other claim a few times! One of our top floor condo units developed a leak in the water supply to the dishwasher and the tenant didn't report it until several hours later. I would estimate at least thirty gallons of water leaked into our unit's kitchen and the ceilings of the condo units below. Needless to say, this was a heck of a mess and there was a lot of water damage! While my insurance company was fairly responsive, they also took a hard stance that ended up costing us some out of pocket expense. They would not cover damages to our neighbor's units as upon their investigation, the insurance company determined no negligence on our part caused the leak.

Which brings me to another lesson learned I want to share using this episode. In matters of liability, one must establish that gross negligence was the proximate cause of the loss or injury. In this particular episode, there was no negligence on my part so our insurance would not pay for our neighbor's damages. As mentioned earlier, I went ahead and came out of pocket to keep the peace, but I certainly was not obligated too.

This same principle holds true for any liability claim. A tenant (or anyone else who may file a law suit) must prove that the property owner's gross negligence was the proximate cause of the damages. Standard rental property insurance policies usually provide for $300000 in liability protection. Additionally, there are "umbrella" insurance policies which I didn't learn about until later in life when our financial advisor suggested we consider additional protection for our assets. Umbrella policies simply add additional liability protection for exposures (think rental properties) above and beyond what is covered in a homeowners or auto policy.

Umbrella policy coverage usually starts at $1 million and work their way up. Fortunately, annual premiums on umbrella policies are not terribly expensive considering the amount they cover. Within the policy, each exposure will be identified and includes properties owned as well as licensed drivers within the household, watercraft, recreational vehicles etc... Once an investor's portfolio starts reaching into the hundreds of thousands, an umbrella policy can add an extra layer of protection for the assets they worked so hard to attain! Between the coverage provided by our rental property homeowner's policy, LLC held properties and our umbrella policy, we feel adequately covered for now.

I'll share another quick lesson I learned about insurance as a result of these two claims. While we have numerous policies with our current insurer, it is certainly a love / hate relationship. Oftentimes their processes and procedures can be maddening. One day I decided to shop around for a new insurance company. That is when I learned about a type of insurance "credit" score.

Bottom line, I couldn't find an insurance company who would insure us due to our low score! Our score was low because we had filed two fairly major claims within two years. Fortunately, the company we are with will still write new policies. Our insurance "credit" score will improve over time assuming no new claims. Something to be mindful of when looking for a policy.

Lastly, a few words on my least favorite type of insurance. Real estate that lies in a flood plain will require flood insurance, especially if there is a mortgage on the property. Regular rental property homeowner's policies do not cover flood damage. Flood insurance premiums are set by the government and expensive. FEMA designated flood zones are often changing and the maps can easily be found on line to determine if a property lies within a flood plain. Always complete due diligence regarding flood plains when considering a property. Generally, I'd recommend not purchasing investment properties in flood plains, but sometimes it cannot be helped due to very conservative flood area designations made by FEMA in the post hurricane Katrina era. Also if looking for any type of recreational property such as near a lake or ocean, flood insurance will be a requirement.

We purchased a property in central Texas that sat next to a bone dry drainage creek. During the closing process, both the appraisal as well as the bank's flood certification came back indicating the property did not lie in a flood plain. No sooner had the ink dried on the closing documents, the bank notified us that the property did in fact lie within a flood plain and we would need to secure flood insurance.

Our lawyer contacted the bank with our concerns. We had well documented evidence that state licensed service providers chosen by the bank and that we had paid for, indicated the property was not in a flood zone. Turns out, the appraiser and flood cert person were using outdated FEMA maps in their assessment!

Long story short, we were able to work out a compromise with the bank to maintain a "force placed" flood policy on the property for only the amount of the mortgage, not the whole property and contents value which tremendously reduced the insured amount on the policy and corresponding premiums. While this increased our expenses for the property, it didn't cut into our profit margin terribly. We've done well with the investment for the past 10 years and there hasn't even been the slightest hint of flooding.

Even though we had a legal case against the bank or perhaps the appraiser, the moral of this story is buyers are responsible for performing all due diligence prior to the sale. Flood zone should be confirmed by the buyer on the FEMA web site whenever considering a property. Flood insurance is a sometimes necessary cost, but one I'd rather avoid!

I've covered how to grow a real estate investment by protecting from loss, now let's shift to creating efficiencies in the business which can grow profit!

Refinancing

I'll start by saying we probably have not refinanced our mortgages enough over the years. All five refi's we've completed were positive outcomes and increased profitability of our investments. As you may recall in the "get to yes" section, not all lenders apply the same business practices. Many lenders will not refi investment property mortgages for obvious reasons, namely the bank's increased risk. I am certain if I had paid a little closer attention and shopped around for better mortgages over the years, our portfolio would be even stronger than it is now. Refinancing is an excellent way to increase profit over the long haul and thus grow the real estate investment. That being said, mortgage refinancing is not quite as simple as the advertisements would make it out to be.

Knowing when to refinance is probably the toughest factor to nail down. For us, we didn't even consider refinancing unless we could get a minimum of one point lower than our current mortgage. Anything less and the breakeven math (more on that later) usually doesn't work out advantageously. We've refinanced our primary residence twice, once about ten years ago in Texas and again this past December in our current home. During our first refinance, we knew we'd be leaving the area soon and would turn the property (a duplex) into a 100% rental property. Usually, refinancing doesn't make sense if you know you'll be moving soon but there are exceptions as I've just pointed out. In the case of our second primary residence refinance, it was just too good an opportunity to pass up. We dropped nearly two points and lowered our payment by $300! Eventually we hope to convert our current primary residence into a rental someday as well.

Earlier this year we closed on two investment property refinances. I previously inquired with other lenders about refinancing investment property mortgages and either got a "no" or a rate quote that didn't make it worth our time. Not sure if it was luck or timing but we found a lender who gladly refinanced our investment properties increasing our net income on these two properties $300 a month!

Another key consideration when refinancing is amortization. As the borrower pays down a mortgage, the monthly ratio of principal to interest (slowly) increases, thus building equity in the home a little quicker. When refinancing, the amortization resets! The owner will still build equity, but back to a slower rate. Not to mention, the payoff date could slip to the right by several more years.

This again comes back to length of ownership. If it is a forever home or a long term investment property, resetting the amortization is not that big of a deal. If planning to move or dispose of the property within the next five to ten years it might be worth taking a look at an amortization calculator to determine if more equity could be built by sticking with the current mortgage.

When refinancing, the biggest consideration is probably determining the "breakeven" point. Refinancing is not free! Closing costs and loan origination fees can add up quickly. Additionally, the amazing interest rates lenders advertise usually require prepaid interest from 1 to 3 points of the loan amount. The small details they leave out of the advertisements! Of course, one can roll these costs into the mortgage principal, but I personally never liked doing that. Any savings on the monthly mortgage from a lower interest rate could be reduced due to an increased principal.

For three of our five refinances we paid loan costs and prepaid interest out of pocket at closing. Our most recent primary residence refinance was a VA streamlined process and the closing costs were so minimal we just tacked them on to the principal. We didn't bring any cash to closing and will break even in 18 months! Important to mention here that if we ever move to a new home, we will convert our current home to a rental property, while retaining the great refinanced mortgage rate!

Our most recent re-finance, although considered as such, was technically not a re-finance but more accurately, converting a new construction loan to a permanent loan. I shared earlier in the book the challenges we encountered while building a new duplex, but as fortune would have it, when it came to financing, we were able to turn some lemons into pretty sweet lemonade! The property appraised for much more than what we owed to pay off the construction loan, therefore we were able to get some cash out on this mortgage. For this particular refi we also rolled loan costs into the principle as it doesn't make much sense to bring cash to closing when getting cash out. We will use the cash out and a little out of pocket to pay off a mortgage on a Texas property. Coincidently, the one that requires flood insurance I mentioned earlier. Not only will that be one less mortgage payment, we won't have to maintain that horrible flood insurance! Our net profit will "grow" by $300 per month.

Real estate is a long term investment and that is why it is important to consider the break even when refinancing. If rolling closing costs into the principal makes your monthly payment only slightly less, then it will take longer to recoup what was tacked on to the principal. If bringing cash to closing, then it's a little easier to calculate the break even. If saving $150 on monthly mortgage payment and there were $5000 in closing costs, then it will take about three years to break even. Our rule of thumb is maximum of around three years to break even. I think anything more than that starts to introduce a little risk. After crunching the numbers and determining refinancing is the correct move, what to do next?

I've already shared how establishing relationships is critical for real estate investing. This is especially true when it comes to finding the best lender. With the total bombardment of advertising these days, it is hard to know who to choose. I learned early on not all lenders play by the same rules. Most of the time, the ads we see are mortgage brokers who will set up the loan and then promptly sell it off to another entity. In other instances, a homeowner may deal directly with the bank who will hold the mortgage.

Don't settle for bad terms or take the first "no". Take the time to shop around for not only the best rate but also a lender you can trust before refinancing. There are a lot more nuanced ins and outs to refinancing and mortgages in general but I'll spare the details! As I opened with, we haven't had a bad experience refinancing and my only regret is we didn't do it more. In case you missed it, just this year we increased our monthly income through refinancing three investment properties by $600 a month or $7200 per year. Add in the $300 per month we saved refinancing our primary residence (which someday may be converted to a rental) and that is over $10000 increase in net income per year. Pretty decent growth!

Rates may be rising soon but don't stop looking and talking to lenders. Refinancing is a key means to "grow" a real estate investment business.

Hiring a Property Manager

It is hard to put a price tag on time and happiness. As mentioned, my wife and I are about at the threshold for number of properties we can manage while juggling my career and getting two teenage sons through high school and into college. Some folks may be better time managers and able to handle 20 or more properties while still keeping a day job. I think at times in my life, I've probably gotten work-life balance out of whack. I know I've focused too much on work or making a buck rather than what is truly important in life, family. We can't get those moments back.

But what if the real estate bug bites us again in a couple of years, prices drop and it's a great time to buy? While I would be perfectly content to quit my day job and manage real estate full time, that would introduce a lot of risk while trying to put two kids through college. A more logical solution would be to hire a property manager for some or all of our properties to share the burden of labor for this "passive" real estate business.

I've shared at different points in the book how we've had a positive experience partnering with a property manager who takes care of six of our rental units located over 900 miles away. But how would I feel having someone managing a property for us that is right down the street? That is

	Self Managed vs. Property Manager								
	Unit	Gross	P&I	Tax	Ins	HOA/Util	Mang.	Maint	tot exp	Net
1	Top Performing Local Unit A	1050	266	57	26	0	0	75	424	**626**
2	Top Performing Local Unit B	950	266	57	26	0	0	75	424	**526**
3	Top Performing Managed Unit A	1125	298	185	31	0	78	75	667	**458**
4	Top Performing Managed Unit B	1125	298	185	31	0	78	75	667	**458**
	Month	4250	1128	484	114	0	156	300	2182	**2068**
	Annual	51000	13536	5808	1368	0	1872	3600	26184	**24816**

probably the biggest struggle. What we've always tried to do is take emotion out of the equation and look at the numbers. I've mentioned a few times that the math can still work with a property manager. This snapshot is from our current financials shows that our top performing duplex here locally nets about $200 more for the building than our top performer in Texas. This is despite higher property taxes in Texas and of course a 9% monthly management fee. $200 may seem like a lot, but what is personal time worth?

It all goes back to what we've covered since page one. Set goals and develop a plan. It's probably advisable to determine how big to grow before purchasing that first duplex. That is one part of our investment plan we didn't give adequate consideration. Desiring to grow a real estate investment portfolio as big as possible may require some big decisions including quitting a day job or establishing a good relationship with a property manager. If hiring a property manager, real estate can still be profitable there is just more math to consider. Condition of the property, current rents and of course capabilities of the property manager all have to be factored in to the calculus. But it can be done!

When we set about making our initial real estate investment goals back in 2007, I recall estimating that about a dozen units would be about right to realize our dreams. I never thought we would own 17 rental units spread across 10 properties in two states! Our portfolio grew faster than we perhaps intended and we could have certainly done it more efficiently.

We are very thankful and feel blessed to have this opportunity. It is in both of our nature to want to seek more. More family time, more income, just about more of anything! It's been a bit odd lately not looking at the real estate ads for a new opportunity. Perhaps we are at what we called in the Army a "tactical pause," just waiting for the right conditions to jump back in the market. If so, we can just quit paying ourselves and quickly build some capital for our next big thing.

My wife and I are in our early 50s. Still young by today's standards. I can still get into the crawlspace of our properties to fix a leaky pipe but it's not as easy as it used to be! If we never secure another property that is ok. We've been very successful with what we have. Even if we don't purchase another investment property, we will continue to grow by securing what we have and optimizing our financials for the best return possible.

Another reason to love real estate is that growth is almost inevitable. The real estate investor must plan for growth when setting those initial goals!

Chapter 8: Final Thoughts

The general premise of this book is "it worked for me so it should work for you". I fully realize that is a bit naïve but I also know I'm not the only person who has cracked the code. The simple concepts we've covered are tried and true. In fact, there are those who have been much more successful investing in real estate using these same concepts than I. Ask 10 different real estate investors how they do business and you're likely to get 10 slightly different answers but the principles remain the same.

What I've tried to offer over the past 100 pages or so is an honest, upfront look at how one mom and pop rental property investment conducted operations and achieved success. I've provided just about equal examples of mistakes as wise decisions. This was purely intentional; experience is the best teacher and I've learned more from mistakes than the victories! We've made mistakes, yet are still successful. More evidence about the benefits of real estate investing! I hope my unvarnished narrative lends credibility to our story. More importantly, I hope it served as a personal testimony of the financial truth that the worker must collect rent rather than pay it in order to build wealth.

I know we've covered a lot of ground and at times this book may seem more a lesson on why not to invest in real estate! I hope my candid style did not scare a potential real estate investor away! I just can't stress enough that owning real estate is almost a necessity for the average American to build wealth. Whether owning one home or multiple rental properties, the advantages of owning real estate over other investments and especially over paying rent are numerous. In case you forgot, let's review three reasons why one should invest in real estate and how an investor turns a profit.

Real Estate Increasing in Value is Simply a Matter of "Physics"

Simply put, new cars are made every day but there is no more land being produced. The inhabitants of our planet will always need a place to stay. Real estate increasing in value is a safe bet. There maybe a few exceptions such as properties located in an economic down turn area or next to a landfill. Even those locations will someday experience a resurgence!

Rental Properties Offer a Better Return on Investment in the Long Run

I used the example in chapter one comparing a $50,000 investment in a taxable investment account returning 5% annually compounded for 20 years vs. that same 50,000 used to purchase a duplex. The results at the end of 20 years- the taxable investment account is worth around $130k while the real estate investment should bring in over $350k in re-invested rental income and equity. The math is clear, rental properties offer a better ROI than an average mutual fund!

When Actively Managed, Real Estate is a Less Risky Investment than Equities

Key words here are "actively managed". If actively managed, much of the risk associated with rental property investing is mitigated and overall less than the risk we encounter when entrusting a financial advisor or fund manager to grow our hard earned money for us. We can't control what the stock market will do but we do have a level control over our real estate investments when actively managing. At the end of the day, that's what this book has been all about!

Now let's review the three ways real estate makes money.

Rental Income. We covered in some detail the numerous variables that can impact a properties monthly net income. Regardless, a good investment property should produce some level of net income, meaning that the monthly rents collected equal more than the outgo. Growth is achieved by constantly looking to create efficiencies in the operation that will make that net income increase over time. Ideally, any net income earned from real estate is rolled back into other real estate investments or an investment account which makes the profits compound even quicker. Reinvesting net income is a key step to growing a real estate investment portfolio.

Building Equity. Simply put, equity is the difference between what the property is worth and how much is owed to the bank. If you own the property outright, all that equity is yours! Property values will almost always increase and although multi-family property value may not increase as quickly as single family, they are still my personal favorite real estate investment due to the potential for increased net rental income. "Sweat equity" improvements can improve the condition of a property making it more valuable as we covered during the chapter on "maintain the investment".

Tax Benefits. For example, a landlord may collect $10,000 in gross rental income, but after deducting expenses and depreciation for a particular property, the taxable income is MUCH lower. Simply stated, the rental income on which the investor pays taxes is much lower than the income an investor actually puts in their pocket or reinvests! These tax savings add up over time and increase the "earning" power of an investment portfolio. Take those earnings and reinvest! Of course, there is a small catch, we talked briefly about capital gains and depreciation recapture tax that is incurred when disposing of a property. Regardless, the tax savings in the here and now wisely reinvested over the long haul should greatly offset any tax burden down the road. Leveraging the tax advantages of real estate is crucial to successful real estate investing.

In this book I tried to cover what I think are the key tasks for the beginning investor to take the plunge into rental properties. I hope you've taken notes, refer back to the text often! To recap very briefly, I'll just highlight the big takeaways.

Conditions must be set, one can't just willy-nilly put money into real property. This may mean purchasing that first investment later in life, after saving up capital. It almost always means making a real estate purchase based on profitability, not emotion. Keeping credit in good shape and looking creatively at financing options are also key when considering a real estate investment.

Location, location, location is more than just a cliché but an absolute truth when it comes to investing in real estate. We make money from real estate when we buy it. Do the initial market analysis for the area under consideration. When narrowed down to a prospective property, determine expected rental income and required expenses to figure capitalization rate. An 8-10% capitalization rate is optimal!

Although identified as such by the IRS, nothing about rental income is "passive". Treat real estate investing like a part time job or side hustle and it will help keep your mind right for all the ups and downs. Unlike a brokerage account that a financial advisor takes care of, it is incumbent on the owner to maintain not only the properties but also the financial records for a real estate investment. Learn to do it yourself as much as possible. Managing expenses is critical to staying profitable with real estate investing. Simply put, rental property investing is a commitment.

Don't leave money on the table come tax time. Use the tax advantages of rental property ownership as another income stream. Seek help! Smart tax moves are one area where we definitely need a professional. Reinvest your profits and let them compound!

Lastly, real estate investment is an inherently people business from day one. Before that first purchase, establish what values will guide how your rental business will operate. Learn to get comfortable communicating with bankers and real estate agents as well as tenants. Treat tenants with dignity and respect but have a vetting process. Respond to maintenance issues quickly, do not defer. Because real estate investment is a people business, an investor must cover their assets. Homeowner's insurance is a must and there are several other ways to add additional layers of protection from risk.

I often read articles with formulas for building a million dollar net worth by investing aggressively in stocks or mutual funds. While it may work for some, an equities only approach to building wealth ignores what I believe to be a financial truth, owning real estate and not paying rent is essential to build a net worth of a million dollars or more.

Perhaps after reading this book one could argue that with all the "extra" required to invest in real estate, the juice just isn't worth the squeeze. After all, what is our time and quality of life worth? I will gladly take on the debate. I firmly believe the average American won't be able to get financially comfortable working 40 hours a week and just investing in mutual funds as part of their employer's retirement plan. Especially if they are paying someone like me rent every month!

I've spent a lot of time talking in general terms about the success we've had with real estate investing, let me put it in a more personal perspective. Rental property investing has enabled me and my family to have options. Our two children's college is paid for. When I say college, I mean pretty much any educational experience, from the most exclusive four year university to the best trade school. While it would be great if they earned scholarships or other financial aid, we aren't worried about how to pay for it if they don't. As long as they can get accepted, we got tuition covered. They should graduate college with zero student debt, a rarity these days.

Early retirement is within sight for me. I've played out a million different scenarios in my head and in each one there is not an outcome that doesn't include me retiring from my day job by 60 or more likely, much earlier. Early retirement has been one of my personal goals. I watched my mother work until age 67 and vowed to do it different. Our real estate investments, not our retirement accounts is making early retirement a possibility for me.

Most importantly, real estate has become *generational changing* wealth for our family. Often I think we take this expression to mean passing on a huge inheritance when we die but I am not so sure anymore. With the advances in health care, most people live to be really old! Not to sound cold, but will our kids really care if we live to be in our 90s and pass them a large inheritance when they are in their 60s?

Generational changing wealth is less about the sum of an inheritance and more about passing on to the next generation a progressive view on wealth they can use in their adult lives. Our two sons have witnessed the ups and downs of our real estate journey their entire life. They have contributed by working hard to help me paint, mow and repair our rental properties. In fact, my oldest put the work he's done for our rental property business on his college application! They've had "skin in the game". Now they are starting to see a return on the investment as they get close to college.

I told them when they were young if they put in the work to get accepted to an elite college, then don't worry about how to pay for it. Our oldest lived up to his end of the bargain and was just accepted to a great school! Assuming he graduates, he'll already start his adult life far ahead of where I began. Real estate investing enabled this and he knows it.

Real estate investing has given our kids a new perspective on how to look at wealth. Simply put, they equate wealth with real property ownership. While, like most young Americans, they love nice cars, vacations and clothes. However, our children know real estate is where it's at! They also understand buying a home requires planning for the future (a.k.a. setting conditions) rather than giving into immediate wants. They have learned to be super savers like their parents. Will our boys make their first home a duplex like their parents did? Maybe, but I kind of doubt it.

What I think they will do is make owning real estate a core component of their financial journey. I think they will make their first real estate purchase from a practical or financial perspective rather than an emotional one using many of the concepts we've covered in this book. And as already discussed, due in large part to the head start our real estate investments will provide, they should have the means to do so. In my opinion, this is the definition of generational changing wealth as it applies to real estate investing. It is less about a wad of cash in an inheritance and more about establishing a cornerstone for our offspring to build future financial success.

But on the topic of inheritance… Perhaps, I'll develop a revised edition to this book when we do decide to transition away from real estate investing. Or perhaps we will never sell our properties as long as we live. Regardless, by the time our properties are sold (one way or the other) the equity should be worth a few million dollars. If we are still living, we may pay off our debt and roll the remaining millions into an annuity that will pay a fixed payment for the remainder of our lives. If we leave the properties to our heirs to dispose of, then they will reap the profit without the depreciation recapture and capital gains tax (assuming tax law remains unchanged). Either way, in addition to the generational changing benefits mentioned in the previous paragraphs, our heirs should also receive a great legacy when we are gone, thanks to those rental properties!

Finally, I'd like to close with a few words on the general feeling of uncertainty that is gripping many Americans and probably the world as I complete writing this book. In fact, you may be wondering, why release a book about investing in real estate when home prices are skyrocketing, interest rates are expected to rise and a general economic uncertainty grips the land. I will share my observations on these concerns but certainly don't pretend to offer definite solutions. It is truly unique times we are living in!

As I complete this book, we are entering the third calendar year of a global pandemic that has taken millions of lives globally and impacted us all in many ways. "Normal" will be defined completely differently than it was just a few years ago. Similarly, our economy is in an unusual spot. I've talked about it at several points in this book. Rents are skyrocketing but salaries certainly aren't. Even though my wife and I don't rent gouge in our rental business, we've been forced to increase our rents in order for our properties to remain in our rental market class. Yet our applicants are still reporting essentially the same incomes they were less than five years ago when rent was $300 per month less. Somehow, some way, they are still able to pay rent. How is this possible and is it sustainable?

As far as real estate values go, most markets are experiencing an incredible boom. In our particular area, homes stay on the market literally for a few hours before an offer is accepted. This is despite sales prices which are sometimes 20 to 30 percent higher than they were just a few years ago. Rentals are flying off the market equally fast. We can't rent vacant apartments fast enough. When we list a home for rent, we receive an overwhelming response from literally hundreds of qualified prospective tenants. There is a housing shortage in many areas of our nation. How long will this last? Will the bottom fall out on the real estate market?

I also shared some of our scar tissue with building a new property. It took us two years to build a relatively simple duplex design. While the root cause may have been poor project management by our builder, there were some very real supply chain and labor shortages also contributing to the delays. Demand for materials and workers is far exceeding supply despite inflation, increasing unemployment and a global pandemic. How the heck does that work?

The answers to these questions are certainly beyond my level of understanding of economics. My son is starting college next year and has chosen to major in economics. I am hoping he will gain the knowledge to answer these questions for me!

Yet, with all these unanswered questions and uncertainty about our nation's socio-economic future, my wife and I keep plugging away at real estate. Why? Shouldn't we just cash in while the getting is good? More importantly, why should someone who hasn't taken the plunge into real estate yet even consider doing so now?

I'll go back to my realist world view to answer these rhetorical questions. Real estate can be touched and held. It is the antithesis of "crypto currency" or whatever they call it these days. Real estate is almost guaranteed to appreciate whereas the newest trend in smartphones, vehicles or any other technology will inevitably depreciate or perhaps disappear altogether. Real estate is not a passing fancy.

Even if our nation is entering another real estate bubble and home values or rents go down, they won't go away. At a very base level, the real estate investor will always possess shelter for themselves and others to live. Even in the worst case, if a property burns to the ground, the dirt it is built on won't burn. Real estate is a physical constant, unlike crypto, stocks or other investments.

It all comes down to where do you place your trust? In the earth and basic human needs such as shelter or in those wants and desires devised by society? These are the fundamental attributes of real estate which provides a level of comfort to my wife and me in these uncertain times when we question whether to keep going in real estate.

But what about those aspiring investors who haven't taken the plunge yet? Agreeably, it will be harder for the new investor to get into the real estate market today. How can the worker do it? It really comes down to what we covered in chapter 2, setting the conditions. Today's real estate market may require a little more skillful condition setting to include a few more years of building capital to make that first purchase. Home prices and rents may shape the investor's market analysis, influencing where they chose to invest or even live. The principles we've covered in this book still hold true, even within the current market conditions. Now, and indeed any time, is the time to invest in real estate if the *conditions are set*!

I like to remind our two sons frequently that everything, *absolutely everything*, in this life is the result of a *decision*. They will often retort, if someone dies in a plane crash, that wasn't their decision or some other witty counter. Well, the passenger certainly didn't decide the time of their death but they did decide to get on the plane! Another favorite of our kids, I didn't pick my parents, how was that a decision? True, but it was a decision to have you, just not yours! Everything that happens in life is the outcome of a decision.

Real estate investing and building wealth in general requires good decision making, especially for the average worker. Not just which investment to pursue, but wise everyday personal finance decisions. In chapter one, I briefly reviewed the five financial truths that helped guide our personal finances successfully over the years. I'd recommend mastering good decision making about personal finances and investing before making the plunge into real estate. I'd also recommend finding and applying the financial truths that work for you. It is really another condition that must be set before plunging into the real estate market.

Fortunately, humans are blessed with the free will to make good decisions and create opportunities for ourselves. Real estate investing is a decision intensive endeavor. Even if an investor "hires out" all aspects of their business to include management, bookkeeping and taxes, there is still nearly daily decisions to make about the investment. Yet another reason I bristle every time I hear the words "passive income"!

Perhaps the most important decision about real estate is the first one. Should I invest or not? My hope is the experiences, tips and commentary provided in this book from our 14 year rental property investing adventure will enable you to make an informed decision. Hopefully, our story will serve as inspiration for a lifelong commitment to real estate investing.

A final word of warning, real estate investing is addictive! Closing on a new property and securing a signed lease from a tenant is an incredibly rewarding feeling that goes well beyond the satisfaction experienced with other investments. Whether two or two hundred units, real estate investing is more than an investment, it is a small business. Who doesn't want to own their own business? More importantly, in my humble opinion, owning real estate is an absolute necessity for the average person to build wealth.

Made in the USA
Columbia, SC
21 May 2024